CLASSICAL MUSIC
THE 111 GREATEST WORKS

THE COMPLETE GUIDE
TO BUILDING THE ESSENTIAL
CLASSICAL MUSIC LIBRARY

BY JEREMY NICHOLAS & JAMES JOLLY

FROM THE PUBLISHERS OF GRAMOPHONE & CLASSIC FM

CREDITS

EDITOR James Jolly
SUB-EDITOR Martin Cullingford
PRODUCTION EDITOR Antony Craig
ART EDITOR Charlotte Chandler
PICTURE EDITOR Sunita Sharma-Gibson

PRODUCTION MANAGER Ailsa Donovan
SENIOR PRODUCTION CONTROLLER Suzanne Philbin
PUBLISHER Simon Temlett
BRAND MANAGER Rachael Butler

PUBLISHING DIRECTOR Bob McDowell
GROUP DESIGN DIRECTOR Paul Harpin
GROUP EDITORIAL DIRECTOR Mel Nichols
CHAIRMAN & MANAGING DIRECTOR Kevin Costello

© haymarket media group 2009

Printed in the UK by
St Ives Roche
Victoria Business Park
St Austell
Cornwall
PL26 8LX

INTRODUCTION

"After silence, that which comes nearest to expressing the inexpressible is music." Aldous Huxley

There are few things more enjoyable in life than sharing our enthusiasms with others; whether it's for a favourite book, film, holiday destination, restaurant … or piece of music. And the joy of introducing other people to music is that you can share the experience with them. We've been listening to classical music all our lives and still get enormous pleasure from welcoming new people into what can be a daunting, and often confusing, world – there's so much music out there that it's often difficult to know where to start. Well, here's one place! We've consulted, argued, compromised and finally come up with a list of 111 classical pieces (or groups of pieces) that make a perfect foundation for a classical music collection. And why 111? Well, it's the opus number of one of Beethoven's greatest creations, his last piano sonata.

We tell the composers' life stories, we give an introduction to each work and a recommendation for a recording we think you'll enjoy (downloads are signalled by the symbol ➽). And for the adventurous we've made some suggestions for a number of further works you might like to explore.

Welcome to a world of infinite variety with enormous rewards, a world that can quite literally change your life.

Jeremy Nicholas & James Jolly
Autumn 2009

5

Sir John Eliot Gardiner
Conductor
A musician who challenges preconceptions and forces us to listen again, whether in Bach (page 8), Brahms (page 23) or Haydn (page 58)

PHOTO • SAM BARKER

JOHANN SEBASTIAN BACH

Born Eisenach 1685 **Died** Leipzig 1750

Bach has been called 'the supreme arbiter and law-giver of music'. He is to music what Leonardo da Vinci is to art and Shakespeare is to literature, one of the supreme creative geniuses of history. Amazingly, he was essentially a self-taught, provincial musician who achieved only limited fame during his lifetime.

Bach never saw himself as exceptional – just a pious Lutheran artisan doing his best with a gift that was as much a part of him as his unquestioning religious belief. He was nine when both his parents died (his father was a respected violinist) and sent to live with his older brother Johann Christoph. At 15, he gained a position in the choir at Lüneberg where he was able to indulge in every possible musical pursuit, soaking up scores, composing and studying the organ, clavichord and violin. Though Bach led a parochial life, his thirst for every musical experience and willingness to absorb what other composers were involved in, played an important part in the extraordinary diversity of the great music he was to write.

In 1707 he went to Mühlhausen as organist and four months later, at the age of 22, married his cousin Maria Barbara. The following year saw the first publication of a piece of his own music, the cantata *Gott ist mein König*; at the same time he left Mühlhausen to become court organist to Duke Wilhelm Ernst of Weimar where he composed some of his finest organ works. In 1717 came further advancement with the position of music director to Prince Leopold of Anhalt in Cöthen. This was the start of one of his most fruitful periods as a composer, one which saw the appearance of the *Brandenburg Concertos* and the first book of the *Well-Tempered Clavier*.

He was widowed in 1720 with seven children to feed, but the following year married his second wife, Anna Magdalena Wilcken, a daughter of the court trumpeter at

Weissenfels. During their happy married life, she bore him a further 13 children, though no less than six of Bach's 20 children did not survive into adulthood.

In 1722, the Cantor of Leipzig died and Bach was appointed to this prestigious post. It was the job he retained for the rest of his life. His arduous duties as cantor involved playing the organ, teaching Latin and music, writing music for the services of two churches (Nicolaikirche and Thomaskirche) and directing the music and training the musicians of a further two.

The music that flowed from his pen is some of the greatest spiritual music ever written including the Mass in B minor, the *St John* and *St Mathew Passions*, the *Christmas Oratorio* as well as nearly 300 church cantatas. From this period, too, come the *Goldberg Variations* and the *Italian Concerto*. He composed 'For the glory of the most high God alone', as he himself wrote. 'I was obliged to work hard; whoever is equally industrious will succeed just as well.'

By the end of his, life, Bach's eyesight was failing due to cataracts. An operation in the spring of 1749 left him almost completely blind. Ten days later, after feverishly revising his final work, *The Art of Fugue*, he died of a cerebral haemorrhage. He was 65 years old. Bach was buried in the churchyard of St John in Leipzig. No identification marked the spot. Then, in 1895, his body was exhumed and photographs taken of his skeleton. On 28 July 1949, on the 199th anniversary of his death, Bach's coffin was transferred to the Thomaskirche.

7

BRANDENBURG CONCERTOS (1720)

Six perfectly crafted concertos from a master of variety

Bach composed these masterpieces for the Margrave of Brandenburg and made a flowery dedication to him. It is doubtful whether the Margrave actually liked Bach's "Brandenburgs" – he didn't even bother to include them in the catalogue of his music collection. All six concertos have something different to offer: No 1 in F is the most richly scored, No 2 in F is the one with the brilliant high trumpet part, No 3 in G, has only two movements, No 4 in G is the most light-hearted of the set, No 5 in D is almost a harpsichord concerto, while No 6 in B flat is the most solemn.

If you like this, try: Bach's Orchestral Suites • Corelli's Concerti grossi • Vivaldi's Op 8 Concertos • Handel's Op 3 Concerti grossi • Stravinsky's Dumbarton Oaks

The recording

CONCERTO ITALIANO / RINALDO ALESANDRINI
⊙ Naïve OP30412 + ↦
Oft recorded, the six *Brandenburgs* have been lucky on disc – and this lively and imaginative set finds a group of Italian musicians on splendidly vital form. Harpsichordist Rinaldo Alessandrini homes in on the wit, humour, virtuosity and sheer invention in this Award-winning set.

MASS IN B MINOR
(1733-38)

A towering creation that speaks to people of all creeds

The Mass is considered by many to be not only Bach's greatest work but one of the greatest pieces of music ever composed. Yet this most sublime of all choral works was never heard in Bach's lifetime. In fact, it was nearly a century after his death that it received its premiere (in Berlin in February 1834). It's a tribute to Bach's profound spirituality that he, a Protestant, should have felt inspired to write a Mass belonging to a Catholic ritual. It is the personal expression of a devout Christian. Among its 24 mainly choral sections, perhaps the most awe-inspiring are the "Gloria", "Crucifixus", "Sanctus" and "Credo".

If you like this, try: Bach's St Matthew Passion • Bach's St John Passion • Mozart's Requiem • Beethoven's Missa solemnis • Verdi's Requiem

The recording

ENGLISH BAROQUE SOLOISTS, MONTEVERDI CHOIR / SIR JOHN ELIOT GARDINER
⊙ Archiv 415 514-2AH2 + ↦
A superb line-up of soloists join the excellent choral singers – and this is, first and foremost, a choral work – to produce a performance of astonishing vitality. Gardiner clearly has a deep affinity with, and affection for, Bach's music, and the result is a very fine achievement indeed.

BACH ESSENTIALS

Toccata and Fugue in D minor (c1708)

With "Widor's Toccata", this is the most famous piece of organ music ever written. The opening Toccata section is a series of bold, dramatic flourishes with crunching chords followed by the cumulative excitement of the fugue. In fact, the piece probably wasn't written by Bach at all, was almost certainly not conceived for the organ and was probably originally for the violin.

Orchestral Suites 2 & 3 (c1717-23)

Bach composed four orchestral suites: No 2 in B minor is scored for flute and strings, and the last of its six movements is the lively Badinerie (an old, vivacious dance form). The original version of what has come to be known as the "Air on the G String" is the second movement of Suite No 3 in D. Jacques Loussier's arrangement for jazz trio was used for the long-running TV commercials for Hamlet cigars.

Concerto in D minor for two violins (c1730-31)

The most celebrated concerto for two violins ever written and among the finest violin works of the entire Baroque period. The energetic first and third movements contrast with the Concerto's central section (*Largo*). A distinguished writer on music, Ralph Hill, suggested that this wondrous passage of music might be thought of as a translation into musical terms of Sir Philip Sidney's poem: "My true love hath my heart, and I have his / By just exchange the one to the other given…" It is certainly some of the most serene and deeply spiritual eight minutes you will ever hear.

GOLDBERG VARIATIONS
(1741)
One of keyboard music's greatest sets of variations

Count Kayserling, the former Russian ambassador to the Court of Saxony, often stopped off at Leipzig. The Count suffered from insomnia and often asked a young keyboard player named Johann Gottlieb Goldberg to play for him during his sleepless nights. He commissioned Bach to write some music that would be "soft and yet a little gay" for the occasions when he couldn't sleep. Bach came up with a series of 30 variations on a slow, highly decorated sarabande – the famous opening Aria, a theme that Bach had written for his second wife, Anna Magdalena. It is Bach's only set of variations. Goldberg must have been quite a player – he was just 14 years old at the time – for this, one of the keyboard's great masterpieces, is also one of the most difficult to play. It was also the best paid commission Bach ever had.

9

The recording

MURRAY PERAHIA

Sony Classical SK89243 +
Played on the piano, this is a magnificent achievement, combining superb control of the piano with a probing intellect that's also deeply moving. An outstanding performance. (If you fancy the work played on the harpsichord try Kenneth Gilbert on Harmonia Mundi: HMA195 1240)

If you like this, try: Bach's Keyboard Partitas • Bach's Well-Tempered Clavier • Beethoven's Diabelli Variations • Shostakovich's 24 Preludes and Fugues

SIMON
KEENLYSIDE

THE NEW ALBUM FROM GRAMOPHONE AND OLIVIER AWARD-WINNING BARITONE SIMON KEENLYSIDE

SCHUMANN DICHTERLIEBE
BRAHMS LIEDER

SIMON KEENLYSIDE
MALCOLM MARTINEAU

"...THE GREATEST LYRIC BARITONE OF OUR TIME, INDEED ONE OF THE GREATEST OF ANY TIME" BBC MUSIC MAGAZINE

"AS A VOCAL ACTOR HE HAS NO PEER..." GRAMOPHONE

"IN A LEAGUE OF HIS OWN..." THE SUNDAY TELEGRAPH

BARTÓK

One of the 20th century's most important and individual composers, cherished for his intellectual rigour, uncompromising individuality and personal sound world.

Bartók's early years – like his final ones – were spent in economic hardship and poor health. He was shy and highly introverted, a man who remained physically frail all his life. To make up for it, Bartók (1881-1945) had a cast-iron will that brushed aside rejection, incomprehension and failure. He began composing aged nine and at 10 gave his first concert as a "pianist-composer". In 1904, the year after graduating from the Academy of Music in Budapest, he made a discovery that changed his life. Listening to Hungarian folk music galvanised his creative thinking. With his friend and fellow composer Zoltán Kodály, he went on lengthy trips armed with an Edison recording machine and a box of wax cylinders to collect the folk tunes of Hungary, Transylvania and Carpathia, travelling as far afield as North Africa (1913) and Turkey (1936).

All Bartók's subsequent music is imbued with the varied character of his native folk music. From 1907 to 1934 he taught piano at the Budapest Academy while composing music that became ever more austere and experimental. Though it aroused strong opposition in his own country, outside Hungary his reputation grew steadily from a limited number of performances. Bartók saw that after the Anschluss in March 1938 it would be only a matter of time before Hungary fell to the Nazis. Aged 58, he took his wife and family to the United States where he was given a position at Columbia University. He composed and played a few concerts but the American public was indifferent. Isolated, somewhat embittered at the lack of recognition and, worst of all, in increasing pain from leukaemia, Bartók's final completed score turned out to be his most popular, the Concerto for Orchestra.

CONCERTO FOR ORCHESTRA
(1943)
A thrilling exploration of 20th-century orchestral sonority

This five-movement symphonic work is called a "concerto", Bartók explained, because of "its tendency to treat the single instrument or instrument groups in *concertante* or soloistic manner". Apart from its jovial second movement (the scherzo section of the work), the general mood makes a gradual transition from the sternness of the first movement to a lugubrious Elegy (third movement) and an "Intermezzo interrotto" ("interrupted intermezzo") to climax in a fiery and life-affirming finale which begins with bagpipe imitations and ends in a brassy fugue. It was the result of a commission from the conductor Serge Koussevitzky, made at the suggestion of the conductor Fritz Reiner and violinist Joseph Szigeti.

11

The recording

BUDAPEST FESTIVAL ORCHESTRA / IVAN FISCHER

⊙ **Philips 476 7255** + ⮡

A terrifically colourful and thrillingly well-played performance. Iván Fischer and his crack Hungarian orchestra are totally inside this piece and give it a real sense of excitement while remaining totally faithful to the letter of the score.

For a vintage recording, try Fritz Reiner and Chicago Symphony on RCA (09026 61504-2) – an absolutely staggering performance!

If you like this, try: Bartók's Music for strings, percussion and celesta • Bartók's Miraculous Mandarin • Kodály's Concerto for Orchestra • Lutosławski's Concerto for Orchestra

LUDWIG VAN BEETHOVEN

Born Bonn 1770 **Died** Vienna 1827

Beethoven truly felt that he was both sent by God and inspired by God. 'Music is a higher revelation than all wisdom and philosophy,' he is quoted as saying. People approach Beethoven with a feeling of awe and reverence, an appropriate response to one of the supreme creative geniuses of history.

Beethoven had a thoroughly miserable childhood thanks to his alcoholic brute of a father (a singer in the Electoral Chapel in Bonn). Johann van Beethoven and his fellow drinker Tobias Pfeiffer were his son's first teachers; various others contributed to his early musical study of the violin, organ, piano and the French horn. His first work to be published was Nine Variations for piano on a March of Dressler which he composed when he was 12. His first important lessons came from the court organist Christian Neefe, who recognised and nurtured Beethoven's talent. At 14, the Elector Maximilian made him deputy court organist.

In 1792 he studied briefly with Haydn in Vienna, which became his home for the rest of his life. He made his debut there in 1795 after which his reputation as a virtuoso pianist and composer spread rapidly.

Though it remained a secret between his doctor and himself for many years, we know that Beethoven was aware of impending deafness as early as his 26th year. His predicament spurred him to a furious spell of creativity; in the circumstances, it is quite remarkable that he was able to compose such music – of every shape and form, embracing tragedy and joy – without apparent reference to his physical state. Between 1803 and 1808 he presented his Third Piano Concerto and the *Kreutzer* Sonata, his oratorio *Christus am Oelberge*, the *Waldstein*, *Appassionata* and *Moonlight* Sonatas as well as his Symphony No 3 (the *Eroica*). A remarkable document was written about

this time: the letter to the "Immortal Beloved". No one has positively identified which of the many women with whom he had affairs or on whom he had designs it refers to (it's quite possible the "Immortal Beloved" is addressed to all womankind). And still the music came pouring out: the first version of *Fidelio* was given in 1805, followed by the *Razumovsky* string quartets, Symphonies Nos 4, 5 and 6, the Violin Concerto, the Triple concerto and a number of piano sonatas. The inexorable progress of Beethoven's deafness made him increasingly irritable, over-sensitive, scornful and petulant, more inclined to retreat into himself and shun society. Yet one masterpiece followed another – the Fifth Piano Concerto (the *Emperor*), Symphonies 7 and 8, the *Les Adieux* Sonata.

The years 1812-17 saw a marked decline in the amount of music and its adventurousness. Beethoven was totally deaf after 1818, the year in which a third and final phase of his development as a composer began – and with a vengeance! It saw the appearance of the mammoth *Hammerklavier* Piano Sonata and heralded the beginning of arguably his greatest and most productive period, the one which brought the Ninth Symphony (the *Choral*), the *Missa solemnis* and the late string quartets.

In 1826 Beethoven caught a cold while visiting his brother; it developed into pneumonia, then jaundice and dropsy. His death on the afternoon of March 26 came in the middle of a violent thunderstorm. For his funeral, schools closed, people stayed away from work and all Vienna mourned. Schubert was one of the torch-bearers.

BEETHOVEN ESSENTIALS

Violin Concerto (1806)

Beethoven's single essay in the genre is also one of the greatest. Generally it is one of his less combative works – the second movement is ethereal with the lyrical soloist soaring over the orchestral chords – with a sprightly and buoyant finale. You should also try the two slightly earlier Romances for Violin and orchestra, mellifluous and heart-warming.

Fidelio (1814)

Beethoven was less happy writing for the voice and the stage than for any other forms, hence his one opera. Its composition caused him agony – one aria he rewrote no fewer than 18 times and he composed four alternative overtures. The opera is based on a French play by Bouilly called *Leonore* (the name of the heroine and the title of Overtures Nos 1, 2, and 3). Yet here, as in the *Choral* Symphony, he takes the listener beyond the expectations of the medium into another realm. *Fidelio* is more a symphony-drama than an opera proper and can be appreciated on record just as well as in the opera house.

The Late String Quartets: No 12 in E flat, Op 127; No 13 in B flat, Op 130; No 14 in C sharp minor, Op 131; No 15 in A minor, Op 132 (1824-26)

These mystical, often difficult, frequently demanding works are the holy of holies, many regarding them as Beethoven's greatest music in any form. Their style is as different from the three earlier *Razumovsky* quartets as the *Razumovskys* are from the six still earlier Op 18 quartets. Traditional ways of developing themes are abandoned. Instead there are fragments of ideas, sometimes repeated, interrupted or varied. The music is elevated to a spiritual plane not found in any other Beethoven works, so that, in the words of one writer, "there is a kind of peace such as we can never know."

PIANO CONCERTO NO 4
(1806)
Orpheus taming the wild beasts
(Liszt)

This is the one which starts with the piano (five quiet introductory bars), a device unheard of until then. Then there's the second (slow) movement in which the piano has an almost tangible spoken dialogue with the orchestra. No 4 is the most lyrical of Beethoven's five piano concertos and more – it's among the most sublime works ever written for piano and orchestra. For many people this is their favourite from the five concertos because it enters territory unexplored elsewhere.

13

The recording

**ALFRED BRENDEL
VIENNA PHILHARMONIC
ORCHESTRA / SIR SIMON RATTLE**

⊙ Philips 462 781-2PH3 + ↱

When Alfred Brendel returned to record the Beethoven piano concertos for the fourth time he did so in the company of Sir Simon Rattle and the Vienna Philharmonic. Musically and intellectually they are a perfect match, and the music-making has an ease that sounds almost like chamber music on a grand scale. Drama, poetry and imagination are all here, making this performance one of the finest of the cycle.

If you like this, try: Beethoven's Piano Concerto No 5, "Emperor" • Schumann's Piano Concerco • Brahms's Piano Concerto No 2 • Rachmaninov's Piano Concerto No 2

SYMPHONY NO 3
in E flat, "Eroica" (1804)
A symphony that shattered all preconceptions with its ambition

One critic described the *Eroica* as "the greatest single step made by an individual composer in the history of the symphony and the history of music in general". It's really an epic four-movement musical essay on the subject of heroism. Beethoven planned the work as a homage to Napoleon, whom he perceived as a champion of liberty. Legend has it that when he heard that Napoleon had crowned himself Emperor, Beethoven's disenchantment led him to scratch out the name "Bonaparte" from the front page of the manuscript and replace it with the one word "Eroica". More important than any legends attached to this great work, though, is the powerful message that Beethoven wanted to convey to the world.

If you like this, try: Beethoven's Symphony No 5 • Brahms's Symphony No 4 • Tchaikovsky's Symphony No 5 • Mahler's Symphony No 3 • Brahms's Piano Concerto No 1

14

The recording

BASLE CHAMBER ORCHESTRA / GIOVANNI ANTONINI
⊙ Sony Classical 88697 19252-2 + ⯈

It is rare nowadays to come across a performance (here on period instruments) of Beethoven's Eroica Symphony that makes this revolutionary work seem new-minted. The mix of drive and acumen is extraordinary. Here is a musician who understands the *Eroica* from within, dramatically, logistically and imaginatively.

SYMPHONY NO 5
in C minor (1808)
So often heard, it still exercises its power over all ages (Schumann)

Da-da-da-daah. Da-da-da-daah. Perhaps the most familiar opening to any piece of symphonic music, these three short notes, one long, then repeated, have had all kinds of interpretations attached to them. Beethoven's friend Schindler was the first to suggest they represented Fate knocking at the door. It's more probable that they were inspired by the song of the goldfinch. Latterly, it is the fact that three short dots and one long signified the letter V in Morse Code that 'V for Victory' became the effective call-sign for the Allied Forces during the Second World War. Beethoven wrote this great and profound work when he was 38 years old.

If you like this, try: Tchaikovsky's Symphony No 4 • Mahler's Symphony No 5 • Sibelius's Symphony No 5 • Beethoven's Fidelio • Shostakovich's Symphony No 10

The recording

VIENNA PHILHARMONIC CARLOS KLEIBER
⊙ DG 447 400-2GOR + ⯈

This has been the classic recommendation for the past 30 years – and it still has the power to impress, move and thrill. Carlos Kleiber made very few recordings during his life, but if one sums up his dynamic approach this is it. The Vienna Phil sound totally galvanised and the sound merely adds to the thrills. It comes coupled with an equally exciting reading of the Seventh Symphony.

OTHER ESSENTIAL WORKS

Symphony No 1 (1800)
To our ears, an easy, agreeable listen but to contemporary audiences, who had heard Haydn's final symphony only five years earlier, Beethoven's effort was challenging and dissonant.

Symphony No 2 (1802)
Even more than the First, the Second indicates that Beethoven was breaking away from tradition. Written at a time when he first realised he was going deaf, the music does not reflect his inner torment but is generally of a sunny, easy-going disposition.

Symphony No 4 (1806)
Dedicated to the Prince's friend Count Oppersdorff, this symphony requires the smallest forces of all nine, one of almost classical proportions. Berlioz described it as a work of "heavenly sweetness".

Symphony No 6, "Pastoral" (1808)
This hymn to Nature originally bore the title "Characteristic Symphony: The recollections of life in the country." The descriptive titles by which we know its five movements were added later.

Symphony No 7 (1812)
This life-enhancing work was famously described by Wagner as "the apotheosis of the dance" because of the emphasis on rhythmic power that pervades all four movements.

Symphony No 8 (1812)
The Eighth has much in common with the Second, in that both are dominated by joviality and good humour despite being composed in difficult personal circumstances. The finale finds Beethoven at his most mischievous and boisterous.

ANN MARSDEN

SYMPHONY NO 9
in D, "Choral" (1824)
The work that introduced the human voice into the symphony

Beethoven had been attracted to Schiller's *Ode to Joy* as early as 1792; he was making sketches for the symphony from 1815 onwards, but only when he returned to its composition in earnest in 1822 did he finally decide that the finale was the right place for a setting of Schiller's *Ode*. Despite some ungrateful vocal writing in the last movement, the work is a monumental achievement, for the emotional power of the whole score is one of the mightiest celebrations of the human spirit. Its creator never heard it: at its premiere, after the second movement, the totally deaf Beethoven was turned around on the conductor's podium to see the audience's gestures of approval – he had been unaware of the roars of applause behind him.

15

The recording

HELENA JUNTUNEN; KATARINA KARNEUS; DANIEL NORMAN; NEAL DAVIES; MINNESOTA CHORALE & ORCHESTRA / OSMO VÄNSKÄ

⊙ BIS BIS-SACD1616 + ⋺

Vänskä offers a radical rethink of Beethoven's *Choral* Symphony, a youthful, brave statement, free of iconic influences. Considered in purely musical terms, this version would better fit the idea of revolution through renewal. The choral finale moves with wonderful control from a decisive opening to a thrilling and explosive close full of zeal.

If you like this, try: Beethoven's Choral Fantasy
• Beethoven's Missa solemnis • Mendelssohn's Symphony No 2
• Bruckner's Te Deum • Mahler's Symphony No 8

Alfred Brendel *Pianist*
Brendel's fourth recording of
the Beethoven piano concertos
finds him on top form. Read
the review on page 13

PIANO SONATA NO 29

in B flat, "Hammerklavier" (1817)

A work of colossal scope and ambition, the piano's Everest

Actually, all of Beethoven's last sonatas are designated "for the Hammerklavier" (the German word for the piano, as distinguished from the harpsichord) but it seems particularly appropriate for the grim grandeur of this massive work ("as long as a symphony, as difficult as a concerto" someone said – it lasts 45 minutes). Its fugue finale must have been incomprehensible to most of Beethoven's contemporaries. Many pianists feel that the musical and technical demands of the *Hammerklavier* make it the most exacting task for any to undertake.

17

The recording

MAURIZIO POLLINI

⊙ DG 449 740-2GOR2 + ▷

Pollini's two-disc collection of the last five of Beethoven's piano sonatas contains a stunning performance of the epic *Hammerklavier*. In the first movement the astounding technical assurance has you on the edge of your seat with excitement. His controlled vehemence is without rival in the outer movements. This is piano-playing of a truly exalted kind.

PHILLIPE GONTIERE/DG

If you like this, try: Beethoven's Piano Sonata No 32 • Liszt's Piano Sonata • Dukas's Piano Sonata • Sorabji's 100 Transcendental Studies • Alkan's Concerto for Solo Piano

Sir Colin Davis *Conductor*
A great Berlioz interpreter, he's
at his finest in the
Symphonie fantastique

BERLIOZ

The arch-Romantic composer, Berlioz's life was all you'd expect – by turn turbulent and passionate, ecstatic and melancholic

Much against his father's wishes, after abandoning medical studies, Berlioz, aged 22, enrolled at the Paris Conservatoire to study counterpoint and composition. Though he later took up the guitar, unusually for a composer Berlioz (1803-69) never became proficient on any instrument.

In September 1827 he became infatuated with an Irish actress named Harriet Smithson. Over the next three years he worked on a symphony, a gigantic love letter to the object of his affections. This was his *Symphonie fantastique* (see right). It received its first performance at the Paris Conservatoire in December 1830, a date Berlioz timed for the return to Paris of his grande passion. The work was given to great acclaim. After a feverish courtship, Berlioz and Harriet were married in October 1833. The union was not a success.

Throughout the following two decades, Berlioz composed industriously, controversially and increasingly successfully: *Harold in Italy* (commissioned for 20,000 francs by Paganini – though he never played the work), the *Grande symphonie funèbre et triomphale*, the dramatic symphony *Roméo e Juliette*, the *Grand' Messe des Morts* (Requiem) and the opera *Benvenuto Cellini*.

Along the way, his marriage broke up (1841), his dramatic cantata *La Damnation de Faust* (1846) was a failure and his final masterpiece, the gigantic opera *Les Troyens* (1856-58), was on too large a scale to be staged. The final years of Berlioz's life were miserable. The death of his only child (a son from his marriage to Harriet Smithson) came as a final blow.

SYMPHONIE FANTASTIQUE
(1830)
The Romantic symphony par excellence

The innovations and imaginative forces at work in this masterpiece represented a new sound world. Subtitled "An Episode in the Life of an Artist", the composition of the Fantastic Symphony, though closely linked with Berlioz's stormy affair with Harriet Smithson, was based on De Quincy's *Confessions of an Opium Eater* in which a young, sensitive musician with a vivid imagination poisons himself in a fit of love-sick despair. Its five sections trace the hero as he falls in love: Dreams, Passion; The Ball (with its famous waltz movement); Scene in the Country; The March to the Gallows; Dreams of the Witches' Sabbath.

19

The recording

LONDON SYMPHONY ORCHESTRA / SIR COLIN DAVIS

⊙ LSO Live LSO0007CD + ⮕

Sir Colin Davis is the leading Berlioz conductor of our day, a man totally attuned to this complex and deeply Romantic composer's sensibility. He has made numerous recordings of this great symphony and this most recent one finds him and his magnificent LSO (a great Berlioz ensemble) on top form. Few capture the emotional complexity so completely. And it's at budget price!

If you like this, try: Berlioz's Roméo et Juliette • Berlioz's Harold in Italy • Tchaikovsky's Symphony No 5 • Mahler's Symphony No 6 • Prokofiev's Symphony No 5

BIZET

CARMEN
(1875)

'I would go the ends of the earth to embrace the composer of Carmen

(Brahms)

The story of the bewitching dark-eyed gypsy girl who seduces the army corporal Don José and then rejects him in favour of the matador Escamillo has entranced audiences ever since its early performances. It's that rare thing, a truly great work with universal appeal. There are four or five tunes that everyone can sing in the bath: "L'amour est un oiseau rebelle" ("Love is a rebellious bird"), the famous Habañera – though in fact the tune is not by Bizet (he thought it was a folk song and inserted it into the opera only to discover that it was a recently-composed ditty called *El Arreglito* by Sebastián de Yradier, 1809-65), the "Chanson Bohème" – Carmen's wild gypsy dance at the inn of Lilas Pastia – Escamillo's "Toreador's Song", Don José's "Flower Song" and a string of others.

20

It's one of musical history's cruellest blows that after so many doubts and set-backs, Bizet's life should be extinguished at the very point when he had completed the first work of his maturity.

Bizet (1838-75) began his career as a child prodigy on the piano, entering the Paris Conservatoire when he was only nine. He wrote about 150 pieces for the piano, though only his *Jeux d'enfants* for piano duet is still played today. By the age of 17 he had written his accomplished Symphony in C and in 1857 won the coveted Prix de Rome.

Then it all went off course. Throughout the 1860s, Bizet wrote a string of unsuccessful operas. He had an unerring eye for a weak libretto – works like *The Pearl Fishers* and *The Fair Maid of Perth*. By the time he was 30, he had little to show for his early promise.

More aborted schemes followed and then, slowly, it all began to take shape. In his opera *Djamileh* (1871), another failure, many discerned an originality and lyrical gift that hitherto had not been recognised. In 1871 he received a commission from the Opéra-Comique and was able to write to a friend of 'the absolute certainty of having found my path'. This was to be his opera *Carmen*. Meanwhile, Bizet had produced the incidental music for Daudet's play *L'Arlésienne*. Having turned some of the music into a suite, Bizet found he had a success on his hands at last.

But the struggle to mount *Carmen* and the reaction of the first night audience disheartened Bizet further. Fate decreed that he should not live to see his masterpiece acclaimed. On the evening of the 31st performance of *Carmen*, Bizet died of a heart attack brought on by a throat affliction (probably cancer). He was 36. *Carmen* rapidly grew in popularity. Had Bizet lived another few months he would have experienced its total triumph.

The recording

VICTORIA DE LOS ANGELES, NICOLAI GEDDA, FRENCH NATIONAL RADIO CHOIR AND SYMPHONY ORCHESTRA / SIR THOMAS BEECHAM

⊙ EMI 567357-2 + ⏩

Sparkling, swaggering and seducing – this classic set is as thrilling as when Sir Thomas Beecham conducted it half a century ago (only now, having been remastered, it sounds even better). Each phrase is carefully

moulded, while Los Angeles as Carmen proves to be a fabulously seductive, provocative character. Gedda is a passionate Don José, a tenor captured at the height of his powers.

The rest of the cast – mostly French – are an excellent team, making marvellous work of the ensemble moments. The result is a delight.

If you like this, try: • Mozart's The Marriage of Figaro • Rossini's La Cenerentola • Bizet's Symphony in C • Rimsky-Korskakov's Rhapsodie espagnole

JOHANNES BRAHMS

Born Hamburg 1833 **Died** Vienna 1897

**One of the giants of classical music, Brahms appeared to
arrive fully armed, found a style in which he was comfortable
– traditional structures and tonality in the German idiom – and
stuck to it throughout his life. He was no innovator, preferring
the logic of the symphony, sonata, fugue and variation forms.**

At the age of six, Brahms was discovered to
have perfect pitch and a natural talent for the
piano. He made his first public appearance
playing chamber music at 10. As a teenager he
supplemented his income playing in taverns and bordellos.

He began to compose, too, but when in 1853 he met
up with the Hungarian violinist Eduard Reményi, Brahms
leapt at the chance of becoming his accompanist and off
they went on tour. This fortuitous move led to a meeting
with Liszt and life-long friendships with the great violinist
Joseph Joachim and with
Robert and Clara Schumann.
Schumann's diary records their
first meeting with the simply
entry: "Brahms to see me (a
genius)." Schumann introduced
Brahms to his publishers
Breitkopf & Härtel who were to
publish his early works. Brahms's
subsequent relationship with
Clara was probably the most
profound human relationship
he ever experienced. He never
married but sublimated his
love and desire for women in
his music. "At least," he said,
recognising his awkwardness
with women, "it has saved me
from opera and marriage."

Meanwhile, he had written
his magnificent First Piano Concerto (1859). In 1872 he
decided to move from Hamburg and make Vienna his
base. His *German Requiem* and *Alto Rhapsody* from
the late 1860s made him famous but it was the next two
decades which saw the flowering of his genius. Within four
years (1876-80) he had completed his Symphonies Nos
1 and 2 and the Violin Concerto, besides the *Academic
Festival* and *Tragic* overtures. Brahms had much in

common with Beethoven: both were short in stature,
unable or unwilling to have lasting relationships with
women, bad-tempered, and lovers of the countryside;
they even walked about Vienna in the same way with
head forward and hands clasped behind the back. Like
Beethoven, Brahms had an unhappy childhood and was
a prickly, uncompromising man. He nevertheless had a
wonderfully generous side to him when the mood took
him, witness his help and encouragement to young
composers like Dvořák and Grieg. He was a sociable man
who attracted many friends but he
could be quite remarkably tactless
on occasion, blunt to the point
of gruffness and cruelly sarcastic
in later life, characteristics that
didn't make his relations with other
people any easier. After one party
in Vienna, Brahms left saying, "If
there's anybody here I haven't
insulted, I apologise."

In the 1880s, masterpiece
followed masterpiece: the
B flat Piano Concerto, the Third
and Fourth Symphonies and the
Concerto for Violin and Cello. In
the 1890s, he abandoned larger
forms and concentrated on
chamber music and more intimate,
personal piano works, all tinged
with nostalgia and the warm glow
of autumnal romanticism. Perhaps they reflected a growing
realisation of life's transience: it seemed as though all
those who mattered to him were dying and, when Clara
Schumann too passed away in 1896, it affected him deeply.
His appearance deteriorated, his energy disappeared
and he was persuaded to see a doctor. Only months
after Clara's death, he too had gone, like his father, from
cancer of the liver.

21

PIANO CONCERTO NO 1
(1854-58)

Misunderstood at first, this huge work is now a classic

Now one of the cornerstones of the concerto repertoire, it was hissed at its premiere and did not become popular until the 1950s. This was Brahms's first large-scale work (it pre-dates the First Symphony by a full 17 years) and it's conceived on a truly huge scale – it was easily the longest piano concerto to have been composed to that date. Much of the music in the two outer movements is stormy and turbulent, though the wistful second theme of the first movement is immensely touching. Its yearning slow movement comes as a contrast; the inscription on the score, "Benedictus qui venit in nomine Domine", refers to the fact that the music was written in memory of Robert Schumann.

If you like this, try: Brahms's Piano Concerto No 2 • Tchaikovsky's Piano Concerto No 1 • Liszt's Piano Concerto No 2 • Prokofiev's Piano Concerto No 3

The recording

**NELSON FREIRE
LEIPZIG GEWANDHAUS
ORCHESTRA / RICCARDO
CHAILLY**

⊙ Decca 475 7637DX2 + ⮞

This terrific recording (of both piano concertos) won *Gramophone*'s Recording of the Year in 2007, a magnificent achievement by a musician who has been something of a pianist's pianist for years. He steps out into the full public eye here with a huge technique, a poet's sensibility and in the company of a great orchestra and a conductor totally attuned to Brahms's music.

VIOLIN CONCERTO
(1878)

A song for violin on a symphonic scale

Like Beethoven, Brahms was not a violinist, composed just one violin concerto and, in so doing, produced one of the great masterpieces for the instrument. This, as one writer put it, is "a song for violin on a symphonic scale". Brahms's friend Joseph Joachim was on hand to advise, inspire and give the concerto its first performance, but it was seen to be so fraught with difficulties that it was dubbed as a concerto not for but against the violin. Many years later, the celebrated virtuoso Bronislav Hubermann disputed this: "No," he corrected, "it's a concerto for violin against orchestra – and the violin wins!"

If you like this, try: Brahms's Double Concerto • Tchaikovsky's Violin Concerto • Joachim's Violin Concerto • Sibelius's Violin Concerto • Bruch's Violin Concerto No 1

The recording

**JULIA FISCHER
NETHERLANDS PHILHAR-
MONIC ORCHESTA / YAKOV
KREIZBERG**

⊙ Pentatone PTC5186 066 + ⮞

This is a hugely impressive reading of this huge concerto from one of the brightest of the new generation of violin stars, the German Julia Fischer. Kreizberg is a model accompanist and together with his characterful young soloist gives a performance that demands to be heard.

BRAHMS ESSENTIALS

Variations on a theme of Paganini (1863)
The theme is the same Paganini Caprice No 24 in A minor for solo violin that is the basis for variations by Rachmaninov, Lutosławski, Lloyd Webber and others. Brahms described the 28 variations (published in two sets) as "études" and they do indeed cover the entire gamut of pianistic difficulties, as thrilling to hear as they are to play. In performance, many virtuosos omit some of the weaker variations and combine the best numbers from both sets.

Variations on a theme by Haydn (St Anthony Chorale) (1873)
Originally written for two pianos, these orchestral variations have proved to be among Brahms's most frequently heard works. The chorale theme is not actually by Haydn but was used by him in the second movement of an unpublished Divertimento composed in about 1781. It's an old hymn tune (composer unknown) called the Chorale *St Antoni*. There are eight variations played without a break, followed by a finale which is itself an unbroken chain of 18 variations.

Clarinet Quintet (1891)
While on a visit to the Court of Meiningen, Brahms heard the great German clarinettist Richard Mühlfeld (1856-1902) play. It inspired four works: the Trio, Op 114, the two clarinet sonatas, Op 120, and this most cherishable of chamber works. It was composed in Brahms's mountain retreat of Ischl and looks back on his youth and forward, with patient resignation, to death.

TULLY POTTER COLLECTION • SHEILA ROCK/DECCA

SYMPHONY NO 1
(1855-76)
A long time coming, Brahms's First was well worth the wait

"A symphony is no joke," wrote Brahms. He was 43 before he was satisfied with his first attempt at the form. He had written and destroyed many earlier experiments, having been inhibited by what he felt to be the overwhelming greatness of Beethoven. Indeed, Hans von Bülow described Brahms's First Symphony enthusiastically as "Beethoven's Tenth Symphony", praise underlined by the similarity between the second theme of the finale and the "Ode to Joy" from Beethoven's Ninth Symphony ("Any fool can see that," snapped Brahms when someone pointed it out). Also in the last movement, listen out for the tune played by the horns with its resemblance to the clock chimes known as the "Cambridge Quarters".

23

The recording

ORCHESTRE REVOLUTIONNAIRE ET ROMANTIQUE / SIR JOHN ELIOT GARDINER

⊙ SDG SDG702 + ⤷

Heard alongside choral works by Brahms himself and Mendelssohn, this is a towering account of the First Symphony, with high drama and colossal reserves of power. Gardiner is fully attuned to Brahms's musical language and he draws playing of enormous beauty from his period instrument ORR.

If you like this, try: Brahms's Symphony No 4 • Beethoven's Symphony No 6 (Pastoral) • Sibelius's Symphony No 2 • Schumann's Symphony No 2 • Bruckner's Symphony No 4

Julia Fischer *Violinist*
A musician of huge talent whose Brahms Violin Concerto (page 22) belies her years with its majesty and authority

PHOTO • J HENRY FAIR

BRITTEN

Britten came of age in 1934, the year in which Elgar, Holst and Delius died. He rapidly dragged British music into another era – his own.

England's most significant composer in the second third of the 20th century was born on St Cecilia's day. The patron saint of music blessed Britten (1913-76) with precocious gifts. Soon after completing his studies he was commissioned to write the music for a number of documentary films, most notably *Night Mail* for the GPO film unit. In this he collaborated with the poet WH Auden who was to have a significant influence on his thinking. When Auden departed for America in 1939, Britten and his partner, the tenor Peter Pears, followed him, returning in 1942.

Before the end of the war he had produced two of his most enduring works, the *Ceremony of Carols* and the *Serenade for Tenor, Horn and Strings*, but it was his opera *Peter Grimes* that made him internationally famous. In 1948 he, with Eric Crozier and Peter Pears, founded the Aldeburgh Festival. He and Pears made the Suffolk town their home for the rest of their lives together. A string of operas followed *Peter Grimes*, all of which, to a lesser or greater degree, have established themselves in the repertoires of opera houses the world over.

Britten was particularly adept at writing music for children, accessible without being condescending, and works like *The Young Person's Guide to the Orchestra* have had an inspirational effect on generations of young people. In 1961 his powerful *War Requiem* opened the newly-built Coventry Cathedral.

In the last few years of his life, a heart condition reduced Britten to doing very little. Less than six months before his death he became the first composer ever to be elevated to the peerage.

PETER GRIMES
(1945)
The first great British opera of modern times

The work that revitalised British opera – and, indeed, British music – after the Second World War was based on a poem called *The Borough* by George Crabbe. Set in an East Anglian fishing village, the opera tells the grim story of Peter Grimes, a hard, solitary fisherman treated with distrust by the villagers after the death at sea of an apprentice. After a second boy dies, Grimes chooses to take his boat out to sea and drown. The theme of the outsider, of man's struggle against prejudice and unreason was a subject that strongly appealed to Britten for obvious reasons. It was one to which he returned frequently. Four orchestral scene-setters from the opera (the *Four Sea Interludes*) are sometimes heard independently in the concert hall, among the most powerful musical evocations of the sea, cleverly reflecting Grimes's own turmoil.

25

The recording

PETER PEARS; CLAIRE WATSON; JAMES PEASE; GERAINT EVANS; CHORUS & ORCHESTRA OF THE ROYAL OPERA HOUSE, COVENT GARDEN / BENJAMIN BRITTEN

⊙ Decca 467 682-2DL2 + ▷

This 1958 recording with Pears in the title-role has never been superceded in its refinement and insight. With Britten conducting with consummate skill, this is a great operatic recording. All the characters are powerfully portrayed – real three-dimensional inhabitants of The Borough. The sound is still amazingly vivid.

If you like this, try: Britten's Billy Budd • Britten's Serenade for tenor, horn and strings • Britten's War Requiem • Carlisle Floyd's Susannah

VIOLIN CONCERTO NO 1
(1868)

A work that regularly tops the polls of popular classical works

Dedicated to the violinist Joseph Joachim, to whom Brahms was to dedicate his Violin Concerto, the "Bruch G minor" is one of the finest works of the Romantic period and has regularly topped popularity polls. Why? Because it is unapologetically and frankly sentimental in a quite endearing way, because it speaks directly and unaffectedly, because it is expertly crafted and because it is flooded with the most beguiling melodic charm from beginning to end. Each of its three movements are, in their different ways, equally appealing. And it is loved by violinists and the public alike – a sure guarantee of selling seats in concert halls around the world and a work tackled, on record, by every violinist in his or her career.

26

The recording

**KYUNG WHA CHUNG
LONDON PHILHARMONIC
ORCHESTRA / KLAUS TENNSTEDT**
⊙ EMI 503410-2 + ⇨
The art with this much-performed work is to make it sound new-minted each time, and Kyung Wha Chung, in her second recording of the work, does just that. Though made in the studio, this recording has a freshness and spontaneity about it that is more commonly encountered in the concert hall. Tennstedt is a sympathetic and imaginative partner.

If you like this, try: Bruch's Scottish Fantasy • Bruch's Concerto for clarinet and viola • Mendelssohn's Violin Concerto • Spohr's Violin Concerto

BRUCH

Today, Bruch is generally remembered for one work, his Violin Concerto No 1. In a recent poll, its *Adagio* was voted the second most popular piece of all

Bruch had a peripatetic career teaching music in Cologne, conducting and composing all over Germany, moving from Berlin to Leipzig to Dresden and on to Munich. His second opera, *Die Lorelei*, was a success, his choral works even more so. By his mid-twenties Bruch was famous, considered to be the equal of Brahms and a worthy successor to Mendelssohn. Shortly afterwards came the First Violin Concerto.

In 1867 he was made director of the court orchestra in Sonderhausen (his predecessors had been Spohr and Weber) before returning to Berlin three years later. In 1880 he was invited to become the conductor of the Liverpool Philharmonic orchestra and stayed in England for three years. He was tempted to make England his permanent home, but his German accent and quest for teutonic perfection alienated the Liverpool chorus and orchestra. So he moved to America, returning in 1891 to become professor of composition at the Hochschule für Musik in Berlin. By then Bruch was reckoned to be one of the 19th century's major composers. Then it all went downhill.

He was said to be self-centred and dictatorial ("in personal appearance," remarked a contemporary, "Bruch is by no means as majestic as one would suppose from his works"), not the sort of personality to adapt to the new world of Debussy and Stravinsky, especially when his mode of expression was still Mendelssohnian. His son's death in the First World War left him depressed; his choral music fell out of fashion. No wonder this child of the 19th century died embittered, bewildered that his once exalted reputation had shrunk to nothing.

BRUCKNER

Bruckner's reputation rests almost entirely with his symphonies – the symphonies, someone said, that Wagner never wrote.

No one could ever accuse Bruckner (1824-96) of being frivolous, but quite how this unsophisticated, obsequious boor came to write symphonies of such originality and epic splendour is one of music's contradictions. His worship of Wagner verged on the neurotic; his soliciting of honours, his craving for recognition and lack of self-confidence, allied with an unprepossessing appearance and a predilection for unattainable young girls paints a disagreeable picture. The reverse of the coin is that of the humble peasant ill at ease in society, devoutly religious and a personality of almost childlike simplicity and ingenuousness. God, Wagner and Music were his three deities.

The son of a village schoolmaster, Bruckner enrolled as a chorister in the secluded monastery of St Florian where he studied organ, piano, violin and theory. The story of his life until he was 40 was one of continual study, with an income derived from various meagre teaching and organ posts. Few major composers have waited so long before finding their voice. The blinding light of Wagner hit him when he first made the acquaintance of *Tannhäuser* in 1863.

Bruckner was a master organist and it's the organ that makes its presence felt throughout all his symphonies. There are long passages devoted to one combination of sound (as an organist might dwell on a particular choice of registration), sudden changes of texture and climactic sections of huge sonorities – all indicative of Bruckner the church organist. It was not until 1884 that he experienced any success. During the last 25 years of his life, Bruckner combined composition with teaching and he held a number of prestigious appointments in Vienna. Bruckner died a virgin and was buried under the organ at St Florian.

SYMPHONY NO 7
(1881-85)
The work that finally brought Bruckner fame

The first movement of Bruckner's spacious Seventh Symphony opens with a theme that was said to have come to the composer played on the viola in a dream. Sometimes called the "Lyric" Symphony, it is the one that brought him most success in his lifetime. It also contains what is perhaps the high point of his creative output, the second movement *Adagio*. With its organ-like sonority and lasting as long as some entire symphonies from classical times, it was begun in the month before Wagner's death in February 1883 and written in honour of his hero. Legend has it that Bruckner wrote the cymbal crash at the climax of this movement at the moment he heard Wagner had died. After conducting the premiere of the Seventh Symphony, the charismatic Artur Nikisch wrote, "Since Beethoven there has been nothing that could even approach it."

27

The recording

VIENNA PHILHARMONIC / HERBERT VON KARAJAN

⊙ DG 439 0372 + ➡

Bruckner's symphonies sat at the very heart of Karajan's repertoire and over the years he and the magnificent Berlin and Vienna Philharmonics perfected their performances. The Seventh, with its heart-meltingly beautiful slow movement, was one of the works he did superbly. His grasp of a work's architecture gave him the ability to build

this great work, stone by stone – creating a whole that leaves one touched and moved.

If you like this, try: Bruckner's Symphonies Nos 8 & 9 • Mahler's Symphony No 5 • Bruckner's Te Deum • Wagner's Tannhäuser & Parsifal • Britten's Sinfonia da Requiem

FREDERIC CHOPIN

Born Zelazowa Wola 1810 **Died** Paris 1849

Few composers command such universal love as Chopin; even fewer have such a high proportion of all their music in the active repertoire. Yet he is the only great composer who wrote no symphonies, operas, ballets or choral works. His chief claim to immortality relies not on large scale works but on miniature forms.

This greatest of all Polish composers had a French father and a Polish mother, a duality that was to be reflected, consciously or otherwise, in Chopin's music. His first piano lessons were with Adalbert Zwyny and then Joseph Elsner, director of the Warsaw Conservatory. It's largely thanks to them that Chopin developed into the original creative force he became, allowing him to develop in his own way. Having made his public debut at the age of nine, in 1829 he gave two concerts of his own works in Vienna, famously prompting the young Schumann to hail him in print with the words: "Hats off, gentlemen! A genius."

The fading attractions of Warsaw persuaded Chopin to leave Poland in 1830. He never returned. Paris was to be his home for the rest of his life, though initially the Parisians did not take to his playing or music. His destiny was changed by Prince Radziwill who introduced him to the salon of Baron Jacques de Rothschild. Here, Chopin triumphed and from then on his career as a composer (and highly paid teacher) was a story of unbroken success. Chopin was a sensitive, fastidious man who never enjoyed robust health. The rich, privileged world of the aristocratic and wealthy salons not only appealed to his snobbish instincts but provided the perfect ambience for his music and particular style of playing.

He was hypercritical of everything he wrote and the apparently effortlessly flowing melody that we hear played cost him much. There are few works which do not seem genuinely inspired with their seemingly inexhaustible variety of moods and ideas, endless

supply of beautiful themes and poised discrimination. More than any other, Chopin is responsible for the development of modern piano technique and style. His influence on succeeding generations of writers of piano music was profound and inescapable. He dreamt up a whole range of new colours, harmonies and means of expression in which he exploited every facet of the new developments in piano construction.

His first great love in Paris was the flirtatious daughter of Count Wodzinska. Her family put a stop to the affair. His next was perhaps the most unlikely woman of his circle, George Sand, the pseudonym of the cigar-smoking, radical, free-thinking novelist Amandine Aurore Lucie Dupin, Baronne Dudevant. The relationship, more mother-and-son than husband-and-wife, lasted for ten years, during which Chopin was at the height of his creative powers, respected and internationally famous. At the same time, his health deteriorated as consumption took hold.

The increasingly-tense relationship with George Sand came to an end in 1848. A wealthy Scottish pupil of Chopin, Jane Stirling, persuaded him to make a tour of England and Scotland but the stress of the few concerts he played further undermined his health. When he returned to Paris he became a virtual recluse, too weak to compose or teach. Chopin had a good idea of his worth and was determined that only his best work should survive. He gave strict instructions (which were not obeyed) that all his unpublished manuscripts be destroyed. He died on October 17, 1849 from consumption and was buried in Père Lachaise cemetery next to his friend Bellini.

Murray Perahia *Pianist*
One of the undisputed masters
of the keyboard, as at home
in Bach (page 9) as in Chopin
(page 31), or Beethoven,
Mozart, Schubert, Schumann…

PHOTO • MARK HARRISON

PIANO CONCERTOS
in E minor (1829-30) & F minor (1830)

Chopin's largest-scale works combining poetry and power

Chopin's two piano concertos both date from early in his career. The one in E minor was the second to be written but the first to be published and so designated "No 1". In a letter to a friend, Chopin described the slow movement (*Romanza*) as "intended to convey the impression one receives when gazing on a beautiful landscape that evokes in the soul beautiful memories – for example, on a fine moonlit spring night". Introduced by Chopin in Warsaw on March 17, 1830, the Second Concerto has a slow movement (*Larghetto*) which, according to one critic, is "possibly one of the greatest pages ever written by Chopin".

If you like this, try: Moscheles's Piano Concerto No 5 • Mendelssohn's piano concertos • Saint-Säens's Piano Concerto No 2 • Scharwenka's Piano Concerto No 4

PIANO SONATA NO 2
in B flat minor (1839)

A piano sonata approaching perfection

One of the priceless gems of music, this is known as the *Funeral March* Sonata because of its celebrated and sombre third movement, played at every state funeral (usually by a military band). It's followed by a brief final movement in which the whirling right hand plays in unison with the left to create the impression (according to Anton Rubinstein) of "night winds sweeping over churchyard graves". There is something doom-laden and threatening about the opening two movements as well (just listen to the opening bars of the Sonata and the anxiety behind the first theme). Strangely, though, depressed is the last thing you ever feel after listening to the work – just the opposite, in fact!

If you like this, try: Chopin's Ballades • Liszt's Piano Sonata • Schumann's Fantaisie • Brahms's Piano Sonata No 3 • Ravel's Sonatine

OTHER ESSENTIALS

21 Nocturnes (1827-46)

The nocturne is another musical form that Chopin developed. The term was first coined (in piano terms) by the Irish composer and pianist John Field in 1814, but Chopin "invested it with an elegance and depth of meaning which had never been given to it before", as the critic James Huneker wrote. The most popular (probably the most popular of all Chopin's compositions) is No 2 in E flat.

24 Preludes, Op 28 (1838-9)

This extraordinary set of miniatures captures a world of emotion and mood, full of anguish and despair, serenity and tenderness. Most were composed in Majorca when Chopin and George Sand spent an unhappy few months at Valdamossa. Like Bach's 48 Preludes and Fugues, there is one for every major and minor key. Among them are No 15 in D flat – nicknamed the *Raindrop* prelude – and No 20 in C minor on which both Rachmaninov and Busoni wrote sets of variations and Barry Manilow based his hit song *Could it be magic*.

Four Ballades (1836-42)

"Arias without words", "poetic stories" – these are the best ways to describe the four masterpieces for solo piano that Chopin called Ballades. Almost every pianist has (or has had) them in their repertoire.

ETUDES
(1830-40)

Works that raise the idea of a study to new poetic heights

There are numerous books of piano études (studies), each one devoted to a particular aspect of technique (scales, octaves, arpeggios, etc). Chopin's two sets of 12 studies were the first to subsume the purely technical aspects into music of sublime poetry. Perhaps the most loved is Op 10 No 3 (*Tristesse*), a study to develop expression, and turned into a song in 1939 (*So Deep is the Night*); the best known is a study for the left hand – Op 10 No 12 (nicknamed *Revolutionary*, composed in 1831) which a generation of young music lovers first heard played by Sparky (or was it his Magic Piano?). But dip in anywhere and you will come up with a treasure – Op 25 No 1 (known as the *Aeolian Harp*), Op 25 No 11 (*Winter Wind*), for instance, or the two studies in G flat major, Op 10 No 5 (*Black Keys*) and Op 25 No 9 (*Butterfly*).

31

The recording

MURRAY PERAHIA

⊙ Sony Classical SK61885 + ▣➜

This glorious recording won a Gramophone Award: harly surprising given the quality of Perahia's pianism. He marries a real sense of poetry with an intellectual rigour that is perfect for Chopin's music. He traces Chopin's studies back to the music of Bach, and he brings a clarity to the intricate lines, the same clarity that he brings to the Baroque master.

If you like this, try: Chopin's Waltzes • Debussy's Etudes • Brahms's Variations of a Theme of Paganini • Alkan's Etudes • Godowsky's 53 Studies on Chopin's Etudes

CLAUDE DEBUSSY

Born St Germain-en-Laye 1862

Died Paris 1918

Debussy was among the most influential of all the 20th century's composers. His lyrical gift, idiosyncratic harmonies, colours and rhythms, his preference for suggestion rather than direct statement, resulted in a sound world that was quite different from those of Brahms, Wagner and Tchaikovsky, whose music ruled the roost while he was struggling to become accepted.

The refined and exquisitely-coloured music of Debussy came from a man born above his parent's china shop on the outskirts of Paris. After piano lessons with Verlaine's mother-in-law Mauté de Fleurville, a pupil of Chopin, he entered the Paris Conservatoire aged 10 and at about the same time started to compose. Debussy was a strange-looking young man with a bulging forehead (the French call it *un double front*) which he hated and tried unsuccessfully to cover with his hair. His composition teacher, exasperated by Debussy's unwillingness to adopt the traditional method of harmony, enquired what rules he followed. "Mon plaisir," came the curt reply.

After winning the coveted Prix de Rome in 1884, Debussy studied in Italy for three years. Here he met Liszt who introduced him to the music of Lassus and Palestrina (whose austere spirituality rubbed off on Debussy). Back in Paris in 1886, he fell under the influence of Wagner's music (like every other young composer of the time), though with the life-long exception of *Parsifal*, he was to reject it fairly swiftly. Other influences were at work: the eccentric Erik Satie, who encouraged him to write music that was not hidebound by academic tradition; the paintings of Monet, Cézanne, Renoir, Pissarro and others; the symbolist poets Mallarmé, Verlaine, Rimbaud and Maeterlinck; and the Grande Exposition Universelle of 1889, where he first heard a Javanese gamelan orchestra.

If Debussy's music was unconventional for the time, so was his private life. In the late 1880s he met up

with Gabrielle Dupont – "green-eyed Gaby". While they struggled to make ends meet, Debussy wrote a String Quartet (1893) and the *Prélude à l'après midi d'une faune* the following year, the two works with which we may say that Impressionism in music was born. Gradually he began to make a name for himself. After 10 years, Gaby's reward for her support was to be rejected when Debussy left her and married Rosalie Texier – "Lily-Lilo" (as Debussy called her). Gaby Dupont shot herself, survived and disappeared into oblivion. Only five years later, Debussy grew tired of Rosalie ("the sound of her voice makes my blood run cold," he once said) and took up with Emma Bardac, the wife of a wealthy banker. Rosalie Texier, too, shot herself in despair; she, too, recovered. Debussy divorced in 1904 and married Emma in October 1905, the year in which his symphonic sketches *La mer* were first performed. Their only child together was Debussy's adored Chouchou, to whom he dedicated his *Children's Corner* suite. She died in 1919 aged 14.

By the turn of the century, Debussy's music had begun to reach a wider public. His controversial opera *Pelléas et Mélisande*, produced in 1902, won him many admirers and made him internationally famous. His final orchestral works were the set of three *Images* (1905-12) and the ballet *Jeux* (1913) for Diaghilev. From 1909 his health started to deteriorate as a result of bowel cancer and from the beginning of 1918 he could not leave his room and died there at the end of March. Only a handful of his friends were present at his funeral.

DEBUSSY ESSENTIALS

Children's Corner Suite (1908)

Dedicated to his daughter Chouchou, this charming piano suite is in six movements. Among them are "Doctor Gradus ad Parnassum" (evoking memories of piano practice, with a send-up of a Clementi study), "Serenade for the Doll" and "Jimbo's Lullaby" (Chouchou rocking her toy elephant to sleep); the final movement is the popular "Golliwog's Cakewalk" (and it also includes a tune Debussy heard played by the Band of the Grenadier Guards in London and, in the middle section, a sly quote from Wagner's *Tristan and Isolde*).

Images – orchestral suite (1905-10); two piano suites (1905 and 1907)

Though they share the same title and are concerned with tonal impressions, the orchestral and piano suites are unconnected musically. The orchestral *Images* is a colourful three-movement evocation of Spain. In reality, Debussy's experience of Spain was a one-hour stop in San Sebastián, where he went to a bullfight. But the music is more Spanish than any Spaniard could write. The first piano suite, entitled Images, has such masterly miniatures as "Reflets dans l'eau" ("Reflections in the water") and "Poissons d'or" ("Fishes of gold").

La mer (1905)

For all his many musical "water impressions", Debussy was none too fond of sea travel (though he crossed the Channel – the last of these three ambitious symphonic sea "sketches" was completed in Eastbourne). Some critics have condemned the work as formless; after hearing "From Dawn to Noon on the Sea", the composer Erik Satie said "I liked the bit that comes at about a quarter to 11", while one musicologist attempted to explain "Dialogue of the Wind and the Sea" by saying it depicted a sea traveller who gets seasick and finally throws up!

PRELUDE A L'APRES-MIDI D'UN FAUNE (1894)

A ravishing orchestral picture of a sultry afternoon

Inspired by Stéphane Mallarmé's poem of the same title, this famous orchestral work encapsulates the impressionist and symbolist influences perhaps more eloquently than any other of Debussy's works. The poem tells of a faun in the delicious state between dreaming and waking. Debussy describes the work as a prelude: in other words he sets the mood for the poem. An impressionist painter would be more interested in interpreting the impression of the scene in light and shadows rather than its photographic realism; similarly, the symbolist poets would be as interested in the idea of the poem as they would be in the very sound of the words describing the scene. Debussy's beautiful music is entirely analogous with these two schools.

33

The recording

BERLIN PHILHARMONIC ORCHESTRA / SIR SIMON RATTLE

⊙ EMI 558045-2 + ⊳

Rattle steps into competition with one of his great predecessors at the Berlin Phil, Herbert von Karajan. And, like Karajan, he has a wonderful ear for the shimmering, hazy afternoon world of this sleepy faun. Rattle's fabulous Berlin musicians offer wonderfully characterful playing, and the recording (amazingly made live and without a whisper from the audience) is supremely atmospheric.

If you like this, try: Debussy's La mer • Debussy's Syrinx • Ravel's Daphnis et Chloé • Ravel's Shéherazade • Szymanowski's Harnasie • Rimsky-Korsakov's Scheherazade

PRELUDES
(1910 & 1913)
*Debussy's exquisite miniatures
exploit the full range of the piano*

The two sets of piano preludes are a distillation of Debussy's art and also represent the first change of character and technique in piano writing since Chopin. Whereas Chopin's brief masterpieces express clearly defined moods and emotions, Debussy's 24 miniatures resemble improvisatory sketches suggesting "infinitely delicate auditory and visual sensations", as one critic put it. Another point of interest is that Debussy put the title of each prelude at the foot of the page, not at the head – he wanted each piece to be heard as objectively as possible, without preconceptions in the listener's head. The pictures he conjures up are as diverse as "La fille aux cheveux de lin" ("The Girl with the Flaxen Hair"), "General Lavine – Eccentric" (a famous wooden puppet at the Folies Bergère) and "La cathédrale engloutie" ("The Sunken Cathedral") rising from the depths of the translucent sea.

The recording

KRYSTIAN ZIMERMAN
⊙ DG 435 773-2GH2 + ⊡➔
This is piano-playing and recording in the luxury class. Zimerman is the very model of a modern piano virtuoso, vividly projecting the vastly varied character of these 24 miniatures. His almost orchestral range of colour is awe-inspiring and he brings such a wealth of detail to these intricate scores that you discover something new on each listening.

MATT HENNEK/DG

If you like this, try: Debussy's Etudes • Chopin's Etudes • Ravel's Le tombeau de Couperin • Liszt's 12 Etudes d'exécution transcendante • Alkan's Esquisses

DELIUS

THE WALK TO THE PARADISE GARDEN (1901)

An orchestral interlude, often heard on its own, this piece comes between the fifth and sixth scenes of Delius's opera *A Village Romeo and Juliet*. Delius took a little longer than most composers to discover his true musical voice and he finally blossomed with this opera (composed between1899 and1901). *A Village Romeo and Juliet* was first staged in Berlin in 1907 and was given its first British performance by Thomas Beecham in 1910. It tells the story of the love between the children of two quarrelling farmers. From the fair in the Paradise Garden they wander to the river and die together in a barge that sinks as it floats downstream. Not many laughs, but the music is ravishing.

The sound world of Delius (1862-1934) is immediately recognisable – warm, luminous orchestral colours, hazy, impressionistic tone pictures tinged with a romantic glow. He was at his best fantasising, dreaming, drifting – yet its ravishing, luminous beauty is hard to resist.

Julius Delius was a successful Prussian textile industrialist who had settled in the thriving North Country town of Bradford. Frederick (baptised Fritz Theodor Albert and so called until 1904) was expected to follow in his footsteps and in 1882 was sent over to run the orange groves his father had purchased in Solano, Florida. Here he heard the close harmony of Negro singers and realised that music must be his life (the *Appalachia Suite* reflects his time there).

He was greatly attached to Scandinavia (while on holiday in Norway in 1887 he befriended Grieg) but in 1888 he settled in Paris where he remained until 1897. He then moved to the village of Grez-sur-Loin gnear Paris with the painter Jelka Rosen whom he married in 1903. It was to remain his home for the rest of his life.

From the age of 40, the pleasant but derivative pieces of the previous two decades gave way to the distinctive Delius sound in works such as *A Mass of Life, Sea Drift, Brigg Fair* and *In a Summer Garden*, a voice that found a lifelong champion in the conductor Sir Thomas Beecham. By the early 1920s Delius's creative powers faltered. Paralysis and blindness set in, the result of contracting syphilis in Paris in the 1890s. That might have been that had it not been for the intervention of a young Yorkshire musician named Eric Fenby who offered his services as amanuensis to the ailing composer. The painful final four years of his life were alleviated by constant doses of morphine. Delius was buried in 1934 at Grez but was reinterred a year later in the quiet country churchyard of Limpsfield, Surrey.

35

The recording

BBC SYMPHONY ORCHESTRA / SIR ANDREW DAVIS
⊙ Warner Apex 8573-89084-2 + ⇥
A highlight of this fine disc of Delius orchestral works finds Sir Andrew Davis drawing beautiful string playing, full of warmth and depth, from the BBC Symphony Orchestra. Other pieces on the disc include *Brigg Fair* – again, superb string playing – and *In a Summer Garden* in which the delicacy of texture and hazy warmth are difficult to resist.

If you like this, try: Delius's Sea Drift • Wagner's Siegfried Idyll • Elgar's Sospiri • Puccini's Crisantemi • Richard Strauss's Metamorphosen • Barber's Adagio for strings

TULLY POTTER COLLECTION • JIM FOUR/WARNER CLASSICS

ANTONIN DVOŘÁK

Born Mühlhausen 1841 **Died** Prague 1904

If Smetana was the founding father of Czech music, Dvořák was the one who popularised it. A love of the countryside and nature pervades his work. He himself was noted for his sunny, out-going disposition, qualities that are reflected in his music – no turmoil or neuroticism, no dark, brooding side.

If his father had had his way, the greatest of all Czech composers would have followed in his footsteps and become a butcher. Instead his extraordinary musical gifts led him elsewhere, though recognition was a long time coming. He learnt the violin as a child, became a chorister in his native village and played in local orchestras. Financed by an uncle, when Dvořák was 12, he was sent away to study music and learn German.

Throughout the 1860s he was an orchestral violinist and violist, playing in cafés and theatres, and composing prolifically. He played in a concert of Wagner excerpts conducted by the composer himself, falling under his spell, and later played in the Prague National Theatre Orchestra under Smetana. Life was a struggle both financially and creatively. Dvořák lived only for music – and trains (he knew off by heart all the timetables from the Franz-Josef Station in Prague).

In 1873, he abandoned the orchestra for the organ loft (St Adalbert's in Prague), a less demanding job which gave him more time to compose. The same year he married his former pupil Anna Čermáková. Suddenly a string of marvellous pieces appeared (including the Serenade for Strings), news of his music spread and before five years had elapsed he found himself recognised throughout Europe as a major composer. What Dvořák had done was to use the language of Wagner, Brahms and other German post-Romantics and combine it with the musical character and folk rhythms of his native land. Now a fresh, distinctive voice emerged, wedded to his Schubertian gift for melody and felicitous orchestration. In 1874 his Symphony No 3 won him a national prize as well as the respect of Brahms (who was on the competition jury) and the relationship between the two men developed into a lifelong friendship.

Dvořák's frequent visits to England during the 1880s spread his fame further – his choral works were eagerly lapped up – and he was awarded many prestigious honours worldwide, culminating in 1891 with his being made a professor of composition at the Prague Conservatory, awarded an honorary doctorate by Cambridge University and offered the directorship of the National Conservatory of New York at an annual salary of $15,000. Dvořák moved to the States in 1893, after a string of farewell European tours. A combination of homesickness and the discovery of American indigenous folk music inspired a string of masterpieces, including the *New World* Symphony, the Cello Concerto and the *American* String Quartet. On returning to Prague, he resumed his professorship, was made director of the Conservatory in 1901 and appointed a life member of the Austrian House of Lords. During this final period, Dvořák turned to writing symphonic poems based on old Czech legends and, especially, operas – including one (the only one) which remains in today's repertoire, *Rusalka*. His death was marked by a national day of mourning.

36

DVOŘÁK ESSENTIALS

Slavonic Dances, Opp 46 and 72 (1878 and 1886)

These are the pieces that made Dvořák's name internationally famous. They were composed at the request of his publisher, who was hoping to cash in on the success of Brahms's *Hungarian Dances* – and cash in he did. Dvořák originally scored them for four-hands-one-piano but after their initial success made orchestral versions. Where Brahms used original gypsy tunes, Dvořák invented his own and borrowed the dance rhythms of his native Bohemia, like the Dumka, Polka, Furiant and Sousedska. Top favourites are Nos 1 and 8 of Op 46 and Nos 1 and 2 of Op 72.

Piano Quintet in A (1887)

There are three acknowledged masterpieces in this form – one by Schumann, one by Brahms and this. A piano quintet is scored for piano and string quartet (two violins, viola and cello) and this one has four movements, each reflecting Dvořák's preoccupation with the Bohemian folk idiom (you should also try the Piano Quartet in E flat and the *Dumky* Piano Trio from the same period). So it's full of piquant melodies and dance rhythms – a thoroughly sunny, uplifting work.

Symphony No 8 in G (1889)

It's been called Dvořák's "English Symphony" and "Pastoral Symphony", but it's better labelled "Bohemian Symphony" because it's the one that reflects, more than the other eight, Dvořák's national identity. It's such a cheerful piece, described by one critic as "a lovable expression of a genius who can rejoice with the idyllic simplicity of his forebears". The second movement is the most original of all Dvořák's slow movements – a miniature portrait of Czech village life, with birdsong and a rustic band.

CELLO CONCERTO
(1895)
One of the greatest of all cello concertos

While in New York, Dvořák heard the composer Victor Herbert (better known today as the composer of *Naughty Marietta* and a string of other incredibly successful operettas) as soloist in his own Cello Concerto No 2. This provided the inspiration for what is unquestionably one of the greatest works for the instrument. In the second movement you can hear a quotation from Dvořák's song *Lass mich allein*, a special favourite of Josefina Kaunitzová, with whom he had fallen in love 30 years earlier (she later became his sister-in-law) and who died a few months after Dvořák completed the first draft of this masterpiece. He rewrote the ending to incorporate the song again as a memorial to Josefina.

37

The recording

**GAUTIER CAPUÇON
FRANKFURT RADIO SYMPHONY
ORCHESTRA / PAAVO JÄRVI**

⊙ Virgin Classics 519035-2 + ↦

Imaginatively coupled with Victor Herbert's Concerto, Gautier Capuçon's performance of Dvořák's concerto has a wonderful freshness and youthful vitality. This is a performance that takes risks, but they're risks worth taking – a slow tempo one moment reaps huge

rewards, while a slightly faster one the next can be magical. Paavo Järvi's accompaniment is very fine and there are some terrific solos from his fine German orchestra.

If you like this, try: Dvořák's Violin Concerto • Dvořák's "American" String Quartet • Brahms's Double Concerto • Victor Herbert's Cello Concerto

SYMPHONY NO 9 "FROM THE NEW WORLD" (1893)

The first great American symphony — written by a Czech composer

The popularity of the *New World* Symphony has never waned since its very first performance by the New York Philharmonic in 1893. "I felt like a king in my box," wrote Dvořák at the time. The themes are all his own, though he had so thoroughly absorbed Negro folk melodies during his time in America that he convinces you that you're listening to genuine spirituals (listen to the first movement with its echoes of *Swing Low, Sweet Chariot*, and the famous slow movement, later adapted into a pseudo-spiritual entitled *Goin' Home*). American-inspired it may be but there's a strong hint of Bohemian homesickness in the jubilant third and final movements.

38

The recording

BALTIMORE SYMPHONY ORCHESTRA / MARIN ALSOP

⊙ Naxos 8 570714 + ▷

A *New World* from the New World. Marin Alsop launches her music directorship of the Baltimore Symphony with this invigorating and exciting performance. There may have been more subtle accounts but she and her fine players really make this very familiar score sound fresh and new again. There's a nicely poetic undercurrent and, when required, real drama too. At Naxos price this is a bargain that's crying out to join your collection.

KYM THOMPSON

If you like this, try: Dvořák's Symphony No 6 • Dvořák's Cello Concerto • Smetana's Má vlast • Josef Suk's Serenade for strings • Janáček's Taras Bulba

Marin Alsop *Conductor*
She galvanised audiences
in Bournemouth and is now
doing the same in Baltimore.
Her Dvořák *New World*
Symphony is thrilling

PHOTO • ERIC RICHMOND

SIR EDWARD ELGAR

Born Broadheath 1857 **Died** Worcester 1934

Elgar worked firmly within conventional 19th century German harmonic and structural traditions, yet his voice is quintessentially English. His lyrical side conjures up tranquil pastoral beauty; his pomposity and ebullience remind us of the British bulldog – one with teeth.

Elgar was not only self-taught but self-made, in the best Edwardian tradition. His background, belying the military bearing and stiff-upper-lip character in photographs, was one of genteel poverty. His father ran a piano-tuning business from his music shop in Worcester, doubling as the organist. By the age of 12 the young Elgar was deputising for him at the organ and had taught himself (under father's guidance) the violin. Having left school at 15 and determined on some sort of career in music, he gave piano and violin lessons locally and, in 1879, was made bandmaster at the County Lunatic Asylum. During his five years' involvement there, he wrote and arranged dozens of works for this motley ensemble, allowing him to experiment with every kind of instrumental combination at will. He would become an orchestrator of unsurpassed brilliance. Simultaneously, he played in an orchestra in Birmingham and conducted another amateur group in Worcester.

By the time of his marriage in 1889, Elgar was thoroughly versed in the ways of composing and his new wife, Caroline Alice Roberts (one of his piano pupils and the daughter of a retired Major-General) introduced him into moneyed society. It also gave his creative impetus and musical ambitions the boost they needed. All of Elgar's important music was written during his marriage to Alice.

The couple settle in Malvern in 1891. The next 13 years saw the transformation of Elgar from a provincial small-time musician to a great composer of international standing, culminating in a knighthood in 1904. Orchestral and choral works were his main pre-occupations. The success of his religious and secular cantatas *The Black Knight*, *The Light of Life*, *King Olaf* and *Caractacus* paved the way for his 1900 masterpiece *The Dream of Gerontius*. By then, Elgar's name was widely known as a composer of individuality and depth, especially after the appearance in 1899 of another masterpiece, the orchestral portraits of his friends featured in the *Enigma* Variations. By far his most frequently played composition is the military march *Pomp and Circumstance* No 1, premiered in 1901.

Elgar then turned his attention to what he considered to be the pinnacle of the composer's art – the writing of a symphony. He achieved his ambition in no small measure, producing two masterworks, the first in 1908, the second in 1911. A third large-scale work, the inspired Violin Concerto, was premiered the previous year by Fritz Kreisler.

Elgar was awarded the highest British honour for artists, the Order of Merit, in 1911. After his final large-scale choral work *The Music Makers* (1912) and his symphonic study *Falstaff* (1913) he wrote nothing more of importance until 1919: there's a final magnificent autumnal flourish with his Cello Concerto, String Quartet and Piano Quintet and then – nothing. After his wife's death in 1920, Elgar lost the urge to create (he tried hard, though unsuccessfully, to complete a third symphony). He was made Master of the King's Musick in 1924 and given a baronetcy in 1931, but for the last 14 years of his life he was all but silent as a composer.

ELGAR ESSENTIALS

The Dream of Gerontius (1900)

The text for this magnificent choral work was by Cardinal Newman and depicts the death of Gerontius and the journey of his soul towards the judgement seat of God. Elgar transformed it into a powerful meditation on the soul's immortality (it is often described as an oratorio, but the composer disapproved of the description). For many, it's an overwhelming work with its massive forces and three soloists in music that veers from the still and spiritual to the passionate and blazing.

Pomp and Circumstance March No 1 in D (1901)

The middle section (known as the Trio) of this grand military march is the tune to which we sing *Land of Hope and Glory*. Elgar knew it was a winner the moment he wrote it ("I've got a tune that will knock 'em – knock 'em flat," he said) and it's now a second national anthem, but it was not originally conceived to be sung. The words (by Elgar's friend Arthur C Benson) were added a year after the March was premiered, when Elgar used the same melody to end his Coronation Ode composed for the accession of Edward VII.

Violin Concerto (1910)

Elgar's own instrument was the violin – at one time his ambition was to become a soloist – a love that continued all his life. Though slow to be accepted (the solo part is technically very difficult), his Concerto is now admired as one of the finest for the instrument. The score is inscribed, somewhat mysteriously, "Herein is enshrined the soul of…" It was dedicated to the great violinist Fritz Kreisler, who gave its first performance but who, to music's loss, never recorded it.

ENIGMA VARIATIONS
(1899)
A favourite orchestral work with a riddle at its heart

The *Enigma* Variations is a series of musical portraits of Elgar's friends, his wife and himself. The Variations are based on a hidden (enigmatic) theme which Elgar teasingly always refused to reveal. The debate goes on as to whether it is *Auld Lang Syne*, *Rule Britannia*, a theme from a Mozart symphony, all of which have been considered as candidates. If there is a hidden theme (and some are convinced that the "enigma" is an unplayed theme which fits over the opening statement) it doesn't distract from the inspired music. The best known variation is "Nimrod". Why the name "Nimrod"? Elgar loved word-play. His publisher was his friend August Jaeger; the German for "huntsman" is "Jaeger" and in *Genesis* we read of "Nimrod, the mighty hunter before the Lord".

41

The recording

LONDON SYMPHONY ORCHESTRA / SIR ADRIAN BOULT
⊙ EMI 567748-2 + ⊳
Few conductors had a closer relationship with Elgar's *Enigma* Variations than Sir Adrian Boult – he recorded them four times and this one, from 1970, was his last. Everything is judged to perfection, tempos are beautifully controlled and the LSO plays the music not only with burnished tone, but they bring their vast experience with Elgar to bear.

If you like this, try: Elgar's Symphony No 2 • Elgar's Serenade for strings • Vaughan Williams's Fantasia on a Theme of Thomas Tallis • Walton's Symphony No 1

CELLO CONCERTO
(1919)

A work of heart-rending eloquence that speaks directly to the soul

Written at Brinkwells, a cottage near Fittleworth in the peaceful Sussex countryside, this poignant, elegiac masterpiece reflects Elgar's state of mind after the First World War, anxiety over his wife's failing health and other personal concerns. The balance between the solo cello and the orchestra is achieved with supreme sensitivity and, while all of Elgar's opulent, ceremonial style is on display, it is transformed into an introspective essay of sadness and regret which cannot fail to touch an audience. The first performance in October 1919, however, was not a success due to lack of rehearsal but the second was a triumph, featuring a young John Barbirolli as soloist. It was Barbirolli who, 46 years later, conducted the much-loved recording of the work with Jacqueline du Pré as the eloquent soloist.

42

The recording

**JACQUELINE DU PRE
LONDON SYMPHONY ORCHESTRA /
SIR JOHN BARBIROLLI**

⊙ EMI 556219-2 + ▶

This is one of the classic recordings of the stereo era. In 1965, a young Jacqueline du Pré, the veteran Sir John Barbirolli and the LSO went into the studio and produced a recording that spoke to a generation of music-lovers with a power and directness that has never been equalled. This is emotional, touching… unrepeatable.

EMI ARCHIVES

If you like this, try: Elgar's Violin Concerto • Walton's Cello Concerto • Finzi's Cello Concerto • Tchaikovsky's Variations on a Rococo Theme • Tavener's The Protecting Veil

Jacqueline Du Pré *Cellist*
...er recording of the Elgar Cello
...oncerto comes as close as any to
...eing a definitive interpretation

...HOTO • REG WILSON/EMI ARCHIVES

NIGHTS IN THE GARDENS OF SPAIN (1907-16)

Falla's music is imbued with the rhythms and character of Spanish music, though he was strongly influenced by French Impressionist works. Here is Falla's musical impression of the fountains, cypresses, Moorish palaces, orange groves, palm trees and guitars of his native country in the form of a gentle, melancholic piano concerto. It has three-movements: *In the Gardens of Generalife* (the hill garden at Granada with fountains and ancient cypresses), *A Dance is Heard in the Distance* and *In the Gardens of the Sierra de Cordoba*. "If these 'symphonic impressions' have achieved their object," wrote Falla, "the mere enunciation of their titles should be a sufficient guide to the hearer...The music has no pretensions to being descriptive; it is merely expressive. But something more than the sounds of the festivals and dances has inspired these 'evocations in sound', for melancholy and mystery have their part also."

44

FALLA

Felipe Pedrell, the *eminence grise* of Spanish nationalism in music, persuaded Manuel de Falla (as he had Albéniz and Granados) to use his country's character and folklore to express himself in composition. Like Grieg, whose music he greatly admired, Falla preferred not to make direct use of folk melody but to capture the essence and the spirit of his native land as reflected in his own personality.

Falla (1876-1946), the son of a wealthy merchant, was educated privately. When the family moved to Madrid in 1896, he passed seven years of its examinations after just two years of private piano lessons without formally attending the Conservatory there.

He began by writing zarzuelas (popular Spanish light musical entertainments) and won a prize for his opera *La Vida Breve* (Life is Short) (1905). After its success, he decided to go to Paris for a few weeks. Here he befriended Debussy, Ravel and Dukas and stayed seven years. Influenced and greatly encouraged by them, Falla found his own voice and returned to Spain in 1914. This blend of Impressionism and his own ambitions for Spanish music resulted in his three best-known works: *Nights in the Gardens of Spain* and the two ballet scores *El amor brujo* and *El sombrero de tres picas*.

In 1922, Falla settled in Granada. A lifelong bachelor, he was a recluse by nature and went out of his way to avoid attention. All he wanted was to worship God, write music and lead a simple life. At first he sided with Franco during the Civil War but the anti-religious sentiment after the overthrow of the monarchy forced him in 1939 into self-imposed exile in Argentina. He never set foot again in Spain but, after his death at his home near Córdoba, his body was brought back to be buried in the crypt of Cadiz cathedral.

The recording

MARGARET FINGERHUT, LONDON SYMPHONY ORCHESTRA / GEOFFREY SIMON

⊙ Chandos CHAN10232X + ⮑

Pianist Margaret Fingerhut responds splendidly to the changes of mood in a personality-filled performance, wonderfully conducted by Geoffrey Simon – at the end of the work his broadening brings a powerful feeling of apotheosis. Coupled with *El amor brujo,* equally finely played, and featuring mezzo Sarah Walker.

If you like this, try: Falla's Three-cornered Hat • Fauré's Ballade • Debussy's El puerto del vino (Préludes Book 2) • Ravel's Piano Concerto • Chabrier's España

FAURE

The musicologist Paul Landormy observed of Fauré that "his language, always moderate, is like well-bred discourse. He never raises his voice too high. He works in quiet colours. He is most discreet. He leaves much to be inferred. And his reserve is something quite as eloquent as louder outbursts".

What a quiet, undramatic, life Fauré had. Born in 1845, the son of a village schoolmaster, it is said that a blind woman heard the eight year-old boy playing the harmonium and urged his father to take him to Paris to study. Fauré was offered a place free of charge at the newly-opened Ecole Niedermeyer and remained there until 1865, studying latterly with his musical mentor and lifelong friend Saint-Saëns.

After a succession of important organ posts, he landed the most prestigious of all at the Madeleine in 1896, took conducting and composition classes at the École Niedermeyer and become a professor at the Paris Conservatoire. Meanwhile, he married in 1883 the daughter of a successful sculptor.

As a link to the Impressionists and as a teacher of the future generation of French composers, Fauré was of the utmost importance. Eschewing the fashionable habit of Wagner worship, there is an unmistakable "Frenchness" about his songs and chamber work. In larger forms he was unsuccessful but from the mid-1870s his songs, piano and chamber music attracted a growing band of admirers.

Fauré was made director of the Conservatory in 1905, a post he retained for 15 years until increasing deafness made it impossible to continue. All through his tenure he was determined, rather pathetically, to keep his handicap a secret. His final compositions were composed when he was stone deaf. To his son, Philippe, he confided, "For me...music exists to elevate us as far as possible above everyday existence." Quite so. He died in 1924.

REQUIEM
(1888, revised 1893 and 1900)

Fauré's much-loved setting of the words of the Mass for the Dead concentrates on the serenity and tranquility of death, rather than its torment and pain. It is small scale and untheatrical compared with the Requiems of Berlioz, Verdi and Brahms (Fauré tellingly omits the full text of the "Dies irae" – the cue to unleash full orchestral and choral forces – preferring to include only the pleading "Libera Me" section of the text) and yet few would say that the grander scores are more eloquent or moving. Fauré himself was "not a believer but a sceptic" (as his son confirmed) and was inspired to write the Requiem in memory of his father who died in 1885. Its first performance was at the funeral of a well-known Paris architect, a Monsieur Lesoufaché. In this form it had only five sections. Fauré later added the "Offertory" and "Libera me" sections and altered some of the orchestration – this second version is the one generally heard today, though there is also a grander (over-elaborate?) third "symphonic" version.

45

The recording

SOLOISTS, JOHN SCOTT (ORGAN), CAMBRIDGE SINGERS, CITY OF LONDON SINFONIA / JOHN RUTTER
⊙ Collegium COLCD109 + ⮕
John Rutter's performance of his own edition of the 1893 score is fascinating: using a chamber orchestra, small choir and, in the "Pie Jesu", a soprano who could easily be mistaken for a treble (Fauré's own early performances used a boy soloist) is a convincing argument for accepting this score as more 'authentic' than the customary 1900 version and the result is more intimate.

If you like this, try: Fauré's Cantique de Jean Racine • Duruflé's Requiem • Rutter's Requiem • Barber's Agnus dei • Roxanna Panufnik's Westminster Mass

FRANCK

Has there ever existed a milder, more humble man who was also a great composer? César Franck's first taste of acclaim came only months before his death; he didn't seem to mind. His ambitions were simple: to serve music and God with equal reverence. Exceptionally, his creative powers rose instead of declining as he grew older and most of his greatest works were composed in the last four years of his life.

Franck (1822-90) began as a piano prodigy (he was 12 when his father sent him and his brother Joseph, a violinist, off on tour). After the Liège Conservatory, he entered the Paris Conservatoire where his abilities to improvise and transpose on the organ and piano were legendary. Turning his back on a career as a soloist, Franck settled down to a routine that would alter little for the rest of his life: rising at half past five to compose for two hours, teaching pupils all over Paris and playing the organ at various churches. His own organ works are standard repertoire, but you can hear the organ's influence in all his music.

People remembered him rushing from one appointment to another through the streets of Paris, his overcoat several sizes too large for him, his trousers too short, the absentminded, sweet-natured music professor untouched by the lack of worldly recognition. "He possessed the soul of a child," wrote Debussy. He was idolised by his pupils at the Conservatory, where he was made organ professor in 1872. Franck's marriage in 1848 to the daughter of a well-known actress was not a success.

His one taste of public success came in April 1890 with the premiere of his Quartet. Shortly after, he was on his way to a pupil when he was knocked down by a bus. Though he was able to carry on working – he even made it to the pupil's house for the lesson – his physical condition deteriorated and he died of pleurisy.

SONATA FOR VIOLIN AND PIANO (1886)

Franck's Sonata stands alongside the violin sonatas of Beethoven, among the finest in the repertoire. It was written as a wedding present for the renowned Belgian violinist Eugène Ysaÿe and his wife Théophile. Its first performance was played in a room in Brussels in which were some valuable paintings and where no artificial light was permitted. It was a winter's afternoon and after the first movement it was so dark neither Ysaÿe nor the pianist could see the music. They suggested abandoning the concert but the audience would have none of it and demanded to hear the whole sonata (Franck's music very often roused its hearers in this way). So, with a cry of "Allons! Allons!", Ysaÿe and his pianist plunged into the other three movements playing in the dark from memory! It's since become one of the cornerstones of the violin and piano repertoire, known affectionately by violinists as the "Franck Sinatra".

47

The recording

KYUNG-WHA CHUNG; RADU LUPU

⊙ Decca 421 154-2DM + ⮕

Kyung-Wha Chung and Radu Lupu are a fine duo who capture and convey the delicacy and poetry of the Franck Sonata as well as its rapturous grandeur and never can the strict canonic treatment of the great tune in the finale have sounded more spontaneous and joyful.

If you like this, try: Ravel's Violin Sonata • Fauré's Violin Sonata • Debussy's String Quartet • Ravel's Introduction and Allegro • Vaughan Williams's The Lark Ascending

RHAPSODY IN BLUE
(1924)

GERSHWIN

The most frequently performed piece of American 20th-century music was written in the space of a few weeks. Dance-band leader Paul Whiteman, the self-styled "King of Jazz", had asked Gershwin for a jazz piano concerto. Gershwin had declined due to pressure of work (he was busy writing Broadway musicals), when brother Ira spotted a newspaper item announcing George's forthcoming participation in Whiteman's next concert. On the very day that George first played the work through, Ira had been to an exhibition of Whistler's paintings, one of which was entitled *Nocturne in Blue and Green*. The original title of the music, *American Rhapsody*, was changed there and then, encapsulating as it does the European musical elements (Rhapsody) and the American (Blues). Orchestrated by Whiteman's arranger Ferde Grofé, *Rhapsody in Blue* was premiered in front of the musical world's elite with triumphant success. It was one of the first pieces to combine the jazz and classical worlds successfully.

48

No composer has done more to weld the two opposing cultures of serious and popular music together. The works he fashioned with his miraculous melodic gift have stood the test of time and changes in musical fashion, proving to be among the most treasured of all American music.

George Gershwin's father bought a piano in 1910, initially for Ira, his elder son, but it was Jacob (later George) who took to it like a duck to water. Within four years he was good enough to get a job playing popular songs in music shops. Before he was 20 he had written a Broadway hit, *La, La Lucille*. In the score was the hit song *Swanee*. It sold more than a million copies in sheet music and over 2,250,000 records, setting him up for life. An early string quartet went by unnoticed as did a serious one-act opera while he turned out hit after hit musical containing songs like "Fascinating Rhythm", "Lady Be Good" and "The Man I Love", usually with lyrics by Ira.

Gershwin (1898-1937) was possessed with phenomenal energy and ambition and it was inevitable that he should want to prove himself in more demanding music. The bandleader Paul Whiteman provided the catalyst by asking for a concert piece. The result was *Rhapsody in Blue*. It made Gershwin internationally famous overnight. While continuing to write Broadway shows, Gershwin still felt under-educated musically and asked to study with Ravel and Nadia Boulanger. Ravel turned him down. "Why do you want to be a second-rate Ravel," he asked, "when you're already a first-rate Gershwin?"

Other concert works followed (*Second Rhapsody* and *Cuban Overture*) but it was his inspired *An American in Paris* that scored his next success. His folk opera based on the novel *Porgy* by Dubose and Dorothy Heyward was not immediately popular and the acceptance of *Porgy and Bess* as the first great American opera came only after Gershwin's premature death, from an inoperable brain tumor, at the age of 38.

The recording

NEW YORK PHILHARMONIC / LEONARD BERNSTEIN

⊙ Sony Classical 07464 63086-2 + ⇨

Bernstein's *Rhapsody in Blue* is playful and teasing, constantly daring us to try to categorise its style, and then confounding our conclusions. The orchestra captures the authentic flavour of Gershwin's and Bernstein's idiom and Bernstein pushes them to transcend the printed score. The disc also features *An American in Paris*, a performance which swings by with an instinctive sense of its origins in popular and film music.

If you like this, try: Gershwin's Piano Concerto • Gershwin's Cuban Overture • Bernstein's Symphony No 2 (The Age of Anxiety) • Paul Schoenfield's Four Parables

EDVARD GRIEG

Born Bergen 1843 **Died** Bergen 1907

Grieg's music is Norway in just the same way that Elgar and Vaughan Williams are England. It is full of the idioms of Norwegian folk music synthesised with the German Romantic tradition. Like Chopin, Grieg was more comfortable in miniatures than large forms (his early symphony was not a success), used the piano for the vast bulk of his musical expression and fed off a proud nationalism.

Grieg's great-grandfather was a Scot who emigrated to Bergen after the Battle of Culloden, changed his name from Greig and became British Consul there. The music came from Edvard's mother, a talented amateur pianist. Both parents were reluctant to let him pursue a musical career and Grieg, who'd had thoughts of becoming a priest, hated the Leipzig Conservatory where he was sent. It was here that he developed pleurisy, which left his left lung seriously impaired, bequeathing him precarious health and diminished energy for the rest of his life.

In 1863, rather than return to Norway, he went to Copenhagen where the revered Niels Gade, founding father of the new Scandinavian school of composition and Denmark's leading composer, befriended him. Gade inspired him to form the Euterpe Society dedicated to promoting Scandinavian music. This he did with the aid of another gifted young composer, Rikard Nordraak. "From Nordraak," wrote Grieg, "I learned for the first time to know the nature of Norwegian folk tunes and my own nature".

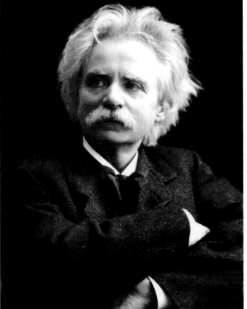

Alas, Nordraak died in 1866 at the age of 24 (though not before he'd written what is today's Norwegian national anthem).

In 1867 Grieg married his cousin, the talented singer Nina Hagerup, who would become the chief interpreter of his songs, but a period of despair ensued: he had found the key to his own musical voice, yet his missionary zeal in promoting Norwegian composers and its music met with opposition; then his first and only child, a 13-month old girl, died in 1869. It was a letter from Franz Liszt not only praising his music but inviting him to Rome that did more than anything to encourage him. After the meeting with Liszt in 1869, he returned to Norway and opened a Norwegian Academy of Music.

In 1869 he gave the first performance of his Piano Concerto, the work by which most people know him. This, together with the first set of *Lyric Pieces* (for piano) and two violin sonatas that had already been published, established him as one of the foremost composers of the time. Ibsen approached him to write the incidental music for the stage version of his *Peer Gynt* (a job which occupied Grieg for two years). In a short time, Grieg had become so famous that the government granted him an annuity to relieve him of financial burdens so that he could concentrate on composing. Ironically, apart from the *Holberg Suite*, all his most successful works were written by the time he was 33.

He was showered with honours and decorations wherever he went, a much-loved figure, but Grieg was a shy, retiring, modest man, a Republican not much impressed by medals and orders bestowed by Royalty. As he grew older, Grieg grew physically weaker and more reclusive, preferring the company of his wife and the tranquillity of his home at Troldhaugen overlooking the Hardanger fjord near Bergen. He died of a heart attack and, following a state funeral, his ashes were sealed in the side of a cliff round the fjord at Troldhaugen.

49

LYRIC PIECES
(1867-1901)
Sixty-six miraculous miniatures that anatomise life

Grieg was essentially a miniaturist, generally at his best in short works such as these 66 piano pieces. Every music lover should have "Papillons" ("Butterflies"), "To Spring" and "Wedding Day at Troldhaugen" (all of which Grieg himself recorded in 1903 in very primitive sound) as well as the five numbers that Grieg orchestrated for his *Lyric Suite*, Op 54 – "Shepherd's Boy", "Norwegian March", "Nocturne", "March of the Trolls" and "Bell Ringing". But dip in anywhere in this collection – there are many more delights than these, and you'll be surprised at how many you recognise.

50

The recording

EMIL GILELS
⊙ DG 449 721-2GOR + ↪

Here's a classic recording, and rarely can a great artist have declared his love with such candour. Gilels discovered in Grieg's *Lyric Pieces* a "whole world of intimate feeling" and managed wonderfully to fuse their intricate mix of innocence and experience. He brings the same insight and concentration to these apparent trifles as he did to the towering masterpieces of the repertoire,

such as the Beethoven sonatas and concertos. This is a disc for everyone's desert island.

If you like this, try: Schumann's Kinderszenen • Tchaikovsky's The Seasons • Ravel's Gaspard de la nuit • Debussy's Children's Corner • Grieg's violin sonatas

Peer Gynt Suite Nos 1 & 2 (1876)

The Norwegian poet and dramatist Henrik Ibsen (1828-1906) asked Grieg to write the incidental music for the first production (in Oslo, then called Christiania) of his verse play Peer Gynt. The title-role was based on a character from Scandinavian legend, a lovable liar and rogue. Grieg was unhappy about the music he composed ("I had no opportunity to write as I wanted") but the result was an instantaneous success. From the two suites he fashioned from the original 23 numbers, "Morning", "Åse's Death", "Anitra's Dance" and "In the Hall of the Mountain King" (all from Suite No 1) have always been firm favourites. The Second Suite, though less popular, has the lovely "Solveig's Song", a haunting Norwegian air portraying Solveig, the bride whom Gynt abducts then abandons but who remains faithful to him. It is typical of Grieg's other songs (he wrote 140 of them), the most famous of which is "Jeg elsker dig" ("I love you") written for his wife Nina in 1865 with words by Hans Christian Anderson.

Holberg Suite (1884)

Norway's greatest composer established almost single-handedly a modern Norwegian school of music, though this work, From Holberg's Time (to give it its official title), written to celebrate the bicentenary of the birth of Ludvig Holberg, is in a Classical style to reflect the era in which Holberg lived. The titles of its four movements reflect this: Prelude, Sarabande, Gavotte, Air and Rigaudon. Holberg (1684-1754), a poet, playwright and philosopher, is regarded as the founder of Danish literature, though he was Norwegian-born and shared Grieg's birthplace of Bergen.

PIANO CONCERTO
(1868)

The work that put Grieg on the musical map

There are many good reasons why this is among the most frequently-played and best known of all concertos. True, it is largely modelled on Germanic Romantic concertos (Schumann's in particular), but from its arresting opening bars to its boisterous finale drawing on the *halling*, a typical Norwegian folk dance, it is a work of white-hot inspiration. The second movement is surely one of the most beguiling in the entire piano concerto repertoire. Grieg was 25 when he wrote this as a vehicle for himself, the first time he had composed anything with an orchestra, and it is his only successful composition in an extended form. He made major revisions several times, the last in 1906, which is the version played today, *de rigueur* for every pianist's repertoire.

The recording

LEIF OVE ANDSNES, BERLIN PHILHARMONIC ORCHESTRA / MARISS JANSONS
⊙ EMI 557562 2 + ▶

It was the Grieg Concerto that first made the name of Leif Ove Andsnes on disc and this later interpretation remains broadly the same, except that speeds are now rather brisker. However many times he's performed the work, Andsnes retains a freshness and expressiveness that always sounds spontaneous. That inspirational quality is more markedly perceptible with the faster tempos here, but the expressive flights remain just as broad. He's firmly supported by Jansons and the Berlin Philharmonic, with playing not just refined but dramatic too when required.

If you like this, try: Grieg's Holberg Suite • Schumann's Piano Concerto • Dvořák's Piano Concerto • Saint-Saëns's Piano Concerto No 2 • Franck's Symphonic Variations

GEORGE FREDERICK HANDEL

Born Halle 1685 **Died** London 1759

Handel is one of the giants of musical history – a great man in physical stature, spirit and vision. His is happy, confident, melodic music imbued with the grace of the Italian vocal school, an easy fluency in German contrapuntal writing and the English choral tradition inherited from Purcell.

Handel's first teacher was the organist of the Lutheran church in Halle, who quickly realised he had a genius on his hands. After three years, he confessed there was nothing more he could teach the boy. Handel was just 11. He doesn't appear to have had any further instruction.

By the time he was 18, people were already talking of "the famous Handel". After a spell in Hamburg, the seat of German opera, he moved to Italy in 1706. The operas and oratorios he composed there were triumphs, and soon "Il Sassone" ("The Saxon") was one of the most talked about musicians in Italy. In 1710 Handel moved to Hanover as court musician to the Elector of Hanover – an astute decision as it turned out. After a year he was given leave to go to England where his opera (*Rinaldo*, 1711) had an astonishing success. Back to Hanover – but London was too tempting and he returned to England.

Two years passed and Handel was still absent from the Hanoverian court. When Queen Anne died in 1714, who should succeed her on the throne but Handel's German employer, the Elector of Hanover.

If George I was displeased with his absentee musician it didn't last long, for soon Handel had a royal pension of £400 a year – with an additional £200 from the Princess of Wales – and was able to embark on a series of operas underwritten by the nobility and cast with the finest European singers. The Royal Academy of Music in London (not the famous music college which came later) was set up to present Italian opera

and the entrepreneurial Handel was made its artistic director. He was, unassailably, the most powerful musician in the land.

By the late 1720s, not long after Handel became a British citizen, public taste for Italian opera waned. Now quite wealthy from shrewd investment, he sank £10,000 of his own money into another Italian opera company and lost the lot. Faced with bankruptcy and the debtors' prison, he wrote himself back into financial success and public favour by resurrecting a genre that was relatively unknown in England – the oratorio. These were dramatised Bible stories set to music, music of the same verve as the operas but with massive choruses and grand orchestral writing. Nothing like them had been heard before.

By 1741, Handel knew he had taken the right direction – public demand was overwhelming. Then in 1742 came *Messiah*, one of history's greatest creative achievements. A succession of other oratorios followed – among them *Semele*, *Judas Maccabaeus*, *Joshua* and *Solomon* – showing Handel to be at the height of his creative powers. The "great Handel" ruled the musical world again, only to be knocked sideways by another cruel blow – blindness. Indomitably, he continued to play the organ and conduct, one of the wonders of London whom people flocked to see and hear.

Handel knew his own worth and asked to be buried in Westminster Abbey – which he duly was, with a statue of him at his work table and the score of *Messiah* open at: "I know that my Redeemer liveth."

52

HANDEL ESSENTIALS

Zadok the Priest (1727)

Handel composed four anthems for the coronation of George II in Westminster Abbey. This one has been heard at every coronation since, sung during the anointing of the sovereign. Its magnificent opening never fails to send a tingle down the spine. The words come from *The First Book of Kings* ("Zadok the priest and Nathan the prophet…anointed Solomon king"). And Zadok? He was a decendant of Aaron and a priest in Jerusalem under Kings David and Solomon.

Organ concertos

High among music's most life-enhancing creations are Handel's organ concertos. The fast movements simply bubble along, contrasted by serene or pompous slower sections. There are 16 in all, most of them written as interludes for Handel's oratorios. Handel was a shrewd businessman-composer as well as being the finest organist of his day. Appearing as organ soloist in the midst of one of his popular oratorios added to his allure and purse. The public lapped it up. The most popular concerto, No 13 in F (*The Cuckoo and Nightingale* because of its bird imitations in the second movement) was composed for the first performance of *Israel in Egypt*.

12 Concerto grossi, Op 6 (1739)

These peaks of Baroque instrumental music were, incredibly, composed in the space of a month: Handel completed the first concerto on September 29, the last on October 30. Even considering that he borrowed some themes from Scarlatti, Muffat, Telemann and (as was his habit) himself, it represents an amazing achievement. And this is not "Baroque wallpaper music". They are the highest manifestation of Handel's compositional skills.

MESSIAH
(1741)
One of the greatest choral creations of all time

"Unquestionably one of the greatest works of its kind ever conceived by the mind of man," wrote one commentator. "In its pages will be found music of both the simplest and most complex nature, but all of it is on the highest plane of inspirational beauty." Incredibly, Handel wrote the entire work in the span of 24 days. This one masterpiece includes "Ev'ry valley shall be exalted", "For unto us a Child is born", "I know that my Redeemer liveth" and "The trumpet shall sound" – as well as the "Hallelujah" Chorus. It was first performed on April 13, 1741 in Dublin. At its London premiere in March 1742, King George II is said to have risen to his feet at the close of the great celebratory chorus. Of course, the rest of the audience followed suit and ever since, in Britain at any rate, it has been the custom to stand for the "Hallelujah" Chorus.

The recording

THE DUNEDIN CONSORT / JOHN BUTT

⊙ Linn Records CKD285 + ↦

For an infinitely rewarding fresh look at Handel's most familiar music, look no further than the Dunedin Consort's performance of Handel's first version, premiered at Dublin in 1742. The score contains some fascinating music we never encounter in more often-heard editions. Everything is

done with a freshness and vitality that is enchanting, the playing sounding

unerringly spontaneous. Harpsichordist John Butt's exuberant direction is meticulously stylish and utterly devoid of crassly pretentious egotism, while choral singing from the group's modest-sized ensemble has terrific punch and illustrates a profound appreciation of text.

If you like this, try: Handel's Israel in Egypt • Haydn's The Creation • Beethoven's Mass in C • Mendelssohn's Elijah • Verdi's Requiem • Elgar's The Dream of Gerontius

ECM NEW SERIES

Thomas Zehetmair   Niccolò Paganini   24 Capricci

Kim Kashkashian
Neharót
Betty Olivero
Tigran Mansurian
Eitan Steinberg

András Schiff   Johann Sebastian Bach   Six Partitas

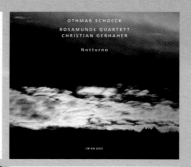

OTHMAR SCHOECK
ROSAMUNDE QUARTETT
CHRISTIAN GERHAHER
Notturno

J. S. Bach
Inventionen und Sinfonien
Französische Suite V
Till Fellner

Heinz Holliger
ROMANCENDRES
Clara Schumann

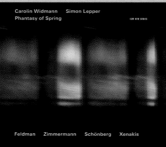

Carolin Widmann   Simon Lepper
Phantasy of Spring

Feldman   Zimmermann   Schönberg   Xenakis

Eleni Karaindrou
Dust of Time
Music for the film by Theo Angelopoulos

K u r t á g o n a l s

László Hortobágyi   György Kurtág jr.   Miklós Lengyelfi

Alfred Schnittke   Symphony No. 9
Dresdner Philharmonie
Dennis Russell Davies

Alexander Raskatov   Nunc dimittis

ARVO PÄRT
IN PRINCIPIO

Ambrose Field
BEING DUFAY
John Potter

Valentin Silvestrov
Sacred Works

Kiev Chamber Choir   Mykola Hobdych

Alfred Zimmerlin
Euridice
Chamber Music

Rolf Lislevand
Diminuito

Available from Amazon
all good record stores
and online retailers

Niccolò Paganini 24 Capricci
Thomas Zehetmair violin

Johann Sebastian Bach
Inventions and Sinfonias
French Suite V
Till Fellner piano

Kurtágonals
László Hortobágyi
György Kurtág jr.
Miklós Lengyelfi

Valentin Silvestrov Sacred Works
Kiev Chamber Choir

Kim Kashkashian Neharót
Betty Olivero
Tigran Mansurian
Eitan Steinberg

Heinz Holliger Romancendres
Clara Schumann

Alfred Schnittke Symphony No. 9
Alexander Raskatov Nunc dimittis
Dresdner Philharmonie
Dennis Russell Davies

Alfred Zimmerlin Euridice
Aria Quartet
Carmina Quartet, Æquatuor

Johann Sebastian Bach
Six Partitas
András Schiff piano

Carolin Widmann / Simon Lepper
Phantasy of Spring

Arvo Pärt In Principio
New Works for Choir and Orchestra
Tõnu Kaljuste

Rolf Lislevand Diminuito
Rolf Lislevand Ensemble

Othmar Schoeck Notturno
Christian Gerhaher
Rosamunde Quartet

Eleni Karaindrou Dust of Time
Music for the film by Theo Angelopoulos

Ambrose Field / John Potter
Being Dufay

www.ecmrecords.com

The recording

THE ENGLISH CONCERT / TREVOR PINNOCK

⊙ Archiv 471 723-2 + ➔

Trevor Pinnock directs the period-instrument forces of The English Concert with great verve and imagination. Clearly energised by Handel's terrific melodic and rhythmic invention, he draws playing of real distinction from these fine players. The disc contains all the music from the three suites of the *Water Music*, and even finds room for an enticing extra, the overture to *Il pastor fido*.

WATER MUSIC
(1717)

Music designed to be heard floating across the River Thames

Three years after George I had ascended the throne, he asked Handel to compose some music specially to accompany a royal pageant on the River Thames. While the royal family were rowed up and down in barges, they listened to a suite of 20 pieces consisting of all kinds of dance music, airs and fanfares. The King liked the suite so much that everything had to be repeated three times. The music wasn't printed until 1741, by which time Handel had added a few more movements. Until recently, the *Water Music* was heard most frequently in the modern orchestral arrangement made by Sir Hamilton Harty in 1922. The second of these is the gentle "Air", one of Handel's best-known tunes.

If you like this, try: Handel's Organ concertos • Bach's Orchestral Suite No 2 • Telemann's Hamburger Ebb und Fluth (Water Music)

55

The recording

LE CONCERT SPIRITUEL / HERVÉ NIQUET

⊙ Glossa GCD921606 + ➔

If you like your Baroque music to thrill and excite this is the recording for you. Hervé Niquet gathered together hundreds of players to try and recreate, with period forces, the spectacle of the first performance. And a mighty sound they make – 24 oboes, 15 flutes and recorders and 14 bassoons make quite an impact! A stunning recording!

MUSIC FOR THE ROYAL FIREWORKS
(1749)

Music of pomp and circumstance

You thought monster concerts in Hyde Park were a recent invention? King George II commissioned Handel to write a suite of celebratory music to be played *al fresco* as part of a huge entertainment in Green Park, London, in April 1749. The rehearsals in Vauxhall Gardens attracted a crowd of 12,000 and the event itself even more. Alas, the gigantic firework display to accompany the music was not a success: the rockets went off alright but the Catherine wheels wouldn't light – except for one which ignited the specially-built wooden Temple of Peace and caused total panic. The music was a triumph, however.

If you like this, try: Handel's Concerti grossi, Op 6 • Vivaldi's La Stravaganza • Mozart's Serenade, Eine kleine Nachtmusik • Stravinsky's Fireworks

JOSEPH HAYDN

Born Rohrau, Lower Austria 1732

Died Vienna 1809

Haydn was among the most prolific of all great composers and he wrote in every form: 104 symphonies, nearly 90 string quartets, 62 piano sonatas, dozens of concertos, oratorios, masses and choral works, 23 operas, many songs and a huge amount of chamber music. His variety, unpredictability, wit, quality of invention and genius for musical construction put him head and shoulders above his contemporaries.

Haydn's father was a wheelwright and the village sexton. Joseph was the second of his 12 children. His extraordinary gifts were spotted when he just six and he was admitted as a chorister to St Stephen's Cathedral in Vienna at the age of eight, yet Haydn never enjoyed a formal musical education.

After nine years of struggling to make a living by playing at social functions, teaching, arranging music and composing, he begun to get noticed and in 1759 was engaged as music director to the Austrian Count Maximilian von Morzin at his estate in Lukavec. The following year Haydn made one of the biggest mistakes of his life by marrying the wrong woman. She had no love of music, nor an appreciation of her husband's greatness, and, though they never divorced, for most of their lives they lived apart.

The turning point in Haydn's career came in 1761 when Prince Anton Esterházy invited him to become Second Kapellmeister at his estate in Eisenstadt. The Prince died the following year, but was succeeded by his fanatical music-loving brother, "Nikolaus the Magnificent", who had one of the most splendid castles in Europe, which included a 400-seat theatre. Here Haydn remained until 1790 and it was here that he composed most of his greatest music. Every week, Haydn and his orchestra had to present two operas and two concerts plus daily chamber music for the Prince. His salary was generous and Haydn was encouraged to compose as he wished.

By 1781 he was acknowledged throughout Europe as a genius, honoured by all. He made only brief

annual visits to his beloved Vienna but on one of them met Mozart for the first time. Mozart was 25, nearly a quarter of a century younger than Haydn. Their mutual admiration and friendship benefited the music that each subsequently wrote.

Prince Nikolaus died in 1791, to be succeeded by his son Paul Anton who was more interested in paintings than music. Still, an annuity kept Haydn as the nominal Kapellmeister at Esterházy while allowing him to live permanently in Vienna. The same year, the enterprising impresario Johann Peter Salomon invited Haydn to London for a series of concerts. He was feted wherever he went and returned to Vienna 18 months later with a small fortune. In 1794 Haydn made a second visit to England, returning later that year to Esterházy. Paul Anton had died, succeeded by his son (another Prince Nikolaus), who revived the Haydn orchestra. As Kapellmeister, Haydn now turned his attention to choral works. From this period come the *Nelson* Mass, *The Creation* and *The Seasons*.

By his mid-sixties, Haydn's health began to fail and in 1802 he resigned as Kapellmeister, though Prince Nicholas II increased his pension and paid all his medical bills so that Haydn should suffer no financial burden. Haydn made his last public appearance in 1808 at a concert given in his honour, conducted by Salieri. The next year, when Vienna capitulated to the French, Napoleon himself ordered a guard of honour to be placed round Haydn's house. When Haydn died, the music at his funeral service was a Requiem by his favourite composer – Mozart.

String Quartets

In the six quartets Op 76 (composed between 1797 and 1798) Haydn's mastery of the form reaches its apex. The D major No 5 is known as the "Largo Quartet" because of its spiritually sublime slow movement. The D minor No 2, is referred to as the "Fifths") because the opening theme of the first movement consists of descending fifths. The C major No 3 is the famous "Emperor" Quartet since it incorporates variations on Haydn's Austrian National Hymn.

Cello Concertos (1783-4)

With over 100 symphonies to his credit, Haydn wrote comparatively few concertos – so far, 24 have been authenticated of which only about half a dozen are heard regularly. The two cello concertos are among them. The one in D major has always been played (the dance-like finale especially represents a real challenge) but the C major is a newcomer. Why? It is only in 1961 that the manuscript was discovered in the Prague National Museum. Rostropovitch was the first cellist to record it in the West and the Concerto quickly established itself in the repertoire.

Trumpet Concerto (1796)

The most popular of all trumpet concertos was composed in 1796 for the Viennese virtuoso Anton Weidlinger. He must have been quite a player for the bustling finale is a real workout for the soloist, even for today's artists who have the advantages of a modern valve trumpet. Haydn wrote this for the keyed trumpet, invented by Weidlinger and which worked by having keys covering holes in the side of the tube. It made it easier for the trumpeter to play all the notes of the scale, but never caught on and was soon superceded by the instrument we know today.

TULLY POTTER COLLECTION

LONDON SYMPHONIES
(1791-5)
A wonderful set of musical visitng cards writen for an English trip

Between 1791 and 1795, Haydn wrote two sets of "London" symphonies, so-called because they were composed for his two visits there. All of them show Haydn at the peak of his creative powers. Haydn himself has been nicknamed "the father of the symphony" and, though not strictly accurate, he certainly developed the symphony to a higher degree than anyone else at the time and showed the way forward. The best known of the 12 symphonies are also the six with nicknames including the *Surprise* (No 94), the *Miracle* (No 96), the *Military* (No 100), the *Clock* (No 101), the *Drum Roll* (No 103) and the *London* (No 104).

57

The recording

LONDON PHILHARMONIC ORCHESTRA / EUGEN JOCHUM
⊙ DG 474 364-2GC5 + ↦
The London Philharmonic Orchestra play superbly and Eugen Jochum gives a series of gloriously cultivated, fresh and often quite enchanting performances. He lavishes great affection on this music and, since it's Haydn, that affection is returned in plenty. Packaged in a little slimline box, this five-disc set is as economical on your shelving as your wallet.

If you like this, try: Haydn's "Paris" Symphonies • Mozart's Symphonies Nos 38-41 • Beethoven's Symphony No 2 • Haydn's "Nelson" Mass • Mendelssohn's string symphonies

THE CREATION
(1796-98)

Haydn in old age imagines the very beginning of our existence

This magnificent, large-scale choral work has some of the most adventurous orchestral writing of the entire 18th century and throughout the following 100 years was Haydn's most popular work. The text is in English, a setting of words from the Book of Genesis and Milton's *Paradise Lost*; the subject of the oratorio is chaos being resolved into order, darkness turning into light. Its opening, depicting chaos, uses a harmonic language literally decades ahead of its time. One of the highlights is the mighty chorus "The heavens are telling the glory of God". Written near the end of Haydn's long life, *The Creation* is a wonderfully assured and ambitious affirmation of faith, but it never loses its very human face – no wonder it has been a choral society favourite for over 200 years.

The recording

SYLVIA MCNAIR; DONNA BROWN; MICHAEL SCHADE; GERALD FINLEY; RODNEY GILFRY; MONTEVERDI CHOIR; ENGLISH BAROQUE SOLOISTS / JOHN ELIOT GARDINER

⊙ Archiv Produktion 449 217-2AH2 + ⤷
This terrific recording does everything a superb performance of *The Creation* should. It thrills, it moves, it surprises, it amazes. Haydn's creativity in his final decade was astounding and this very fine reading brings comparable imagination and technical prowess to bear.

SHEILA ROCK

If you like this, try: Haydn's The Seasons • Haydn's Harmoniemesse • Mozart's C minor Mass • Beethoven's Mass in C • Schumann's Szenen aus Goethes Faust

Holst (1874-1934) is known primarily for The Planets but he wrote lots more. His music owes something to the English folk tradition and the Elizabethan madrigalists and he had visionary qualities similar to that of Vaughan Williams.

Gustav Holst's Swedish great-grandfather settled in England in 1807. His father was an organist and his mother a piano teacher, but when their son (baptised Gustavus Theodore von Holst) went to study at the Royal College of Music in 1893 (where he was a pupil of Stanford for composition), the trombone became his main instrument. Fellow student Vaughan Williams became a lifelong friend. At first Holst earned his living as a trombonist with various theatres and opera companies, then in 1905 he became a teacher at two London schools, St Paul's Girls' School and Morley College – positions he held for the rest of his life.

His early work is dominated by the influence of Wagner, then, tempered by his interest in religious philosophy, by the mysticism, poetry and spiritualism of the East. Vaughan Williams introduced him to English folk music. By 1915 he'd found a voice of his own.

During the First World War he went out to Salonika and Constantinople to organise concerts for the British troops. The Planets, written between 1914 and 1916, did not receive its first complete public performance until 1920, but it established his name as a leading composer.

In February 1923 he suffered concussion after a fall, which led to a rapid deterioration in his health (never robust), which thereafter severely limited all his musical activities except composition. His daughter Imogen, also a musician, said he "sank into a cold region of utter despair...a grey isolation".

FERRECHT MUSIC & ARTS • NICK WITHEROOM

THE PLANETS
(1914-16)

such an overwhelming work that all else pales into insignificance

One of English music's 20th-century masterpieces, this seven-movement orchestral suite was suggested (in Holst's words) "by the astrological significance of the planets". They are not intended to portray the deities after whom they are named. The subtitle of each section confirms what Holst meant: "Mars, the Bringer of War"; "Venus, the Bringer of Peace"; "Mercury, the Winged Messenger"; "Jupiter, the Bringer of Jollity"; "Saturn, the Bringer of Old Age"; "Uranus, the Magician"; "Neptune, the Mystic". (Pluto, which lost its official status as a planet in 2006, had not been discovered when Holst wrote *The Planets*.) This is a work with dramatic, lyrical, emotional, ethereal and coruscating orchestral effects. The best-known section is "Jupiter" which contains the tune known as *Thaxted*, to which we sing the hymn "I Vow to Thee, my country".

59

The recording

MONTREAL SYMPHONY CHORUS (WOMEN'S VOICES) AND ORCHESTRA / CHARLES DUTOIT

⊙ Decca 476 1724 + ↦

Throughout *The Planets*, the invention is as memorable as the vivid orchestration is full of infinite detail. No recording can reveal it all but Dutoit's comes the closest to doing so, creating a whole that leaves one touched and moved.

Consider also Simon Rattle on EMI (359382-2), whose spectacular new recording includes Colin Matthews's *Pluto*.

If you like this, try: Holst's The Perfect Fool • Colin Matthews's Pluto, The Renewer • Holst's The Mystic Trumpeter • Vaughan Williams's Symphony No 6

FRANZ LISZT

Born Raiding, Hungary 1811

Died Bayreuth 1886

Composer, teacher, Abbé, Casanova, writer, sage, pioneer and champion of new music, philanthropist, philosopher and one of the greatest pianists in history, Liszt was the very embodiment of the Romantic spirit. He worked in every field of music except ballet and opera and to each field he contributed a significant development.

Liszt was a child prodigy pianist. When his mother and ambitious father moved to Vienna in 1821 for his musical education, his illustrious teacher Carl Czerny refused to accept payment for the pleasure of teaching the Hungarian wunderkind. By 1824 he was hailed as one of the finest pianists ever heard; by the age of 16 he was famous throughout Europe and financially self-sufficient.

In Paris he befriended Berlioz and Chopin, but it was the electrifying effect of seeing Paganini and the spectacular demands of his violin music that immediately fired his imagination. Liszt set about systematically emulating on the piano what Paganini had achieved on the violin. Between 1831 and 1833, Liszt shut himself away to master his objectives. His re-emergence on the concert platform was a major artistic event and the pianistic artillery he had acquired swept all rivals aside. For the next 14 years he toured all over the continent amassing a fortune. From 1833 he lived with the beautiful Countess Marie d'Agoult. Of their three children, Cosima became the wife of Hans von Bülow and then Wagner. Then in 1847, at the height of his powers, Liszt changed direction.

His new mistress, the Princess Carolyn Sayn-Wittgenstein, abandoned her husband and 30,000 serfs to join Liszt in Weimar where he had been appointed Kapellmeister to the Grand Duke. By the end of the 1850s, Liszt had transformed the town into one of Europe's greatest musical centres. Musicians flocked to Weimar like pilgrims to Mecca. The works Liszt presented and conducted were of the widest variety, from premieres of new and experimental works to high-quality revivals of the classic repertoire.

Astonishingly this period was the one in which the majority of his music was written. The amount he produced is staggering and includes 12 symphonic poems (a form he invented), the *Faust* and *Dante* symphonies, two piano concertos and the *Totentanz* for piano and orchestra, the great B minor Piano Sonata and hundreds of other pieces for the piano as well as revisions of all the piano music he had written in the 1830s and '40s. Moving to Rome in 1860, he took minor orders in 1865, becoming the Abbé Liszt.

From then on he divided his time between his religious interests in Rome and teaching piano in Pesth and Weimar, never asking for a fee. The number of important composers of the next generation whom he advised and encouraged runs into hundreds; the letters he wrote run into thousands (all in his own hand – he never employed a secretary). He reviewed, he gave concerts, he continued to compose. One is left gasping.

Towards the end of his life, the great pianist Moriz Rosenthal, one of Liszt's pupils, commented: "He was more wonderful than anybody I have ever known."

His final triumph was a visit to England in 1886. Though aged and suffering from dropsy, he gave some public concerts. From there he travelled to Bayreuth for the festival. During a performance of *Tristan and Isolde* he had to be taken from the auditorium: pneumonia had set in, swiftly followed by congestion of the lungs.

60

Années de pèlerinage: Book 1 – Switzerland (1848-54); Book 2 – Italy (1837-49); Book 3 (1867-77)

These three books of piano tone poems, the results of Liszt's travels all over Europe, can be compared to an artist like Turner sketching his impressions of the sights and sounds he encountered and then producing a properly-worked canvas as a masterly souvenir. Book 1 of "Years of Pilgrimage" contains one of the finest musical evocations of water in *Au bord d'une source* and a woefully under-rated masterpiece, *Vallé d'Obermann*. Book 2 is inspired by the paintings of Michelangelo and Raphael, the Sonnets of Petrarch and Dante. Book 3 is less inspired but has another remarkable water painting that anticipates the impressionism of Debussy – *Les jeux d'eau à la Villa d'Este*.

Totentanz (1849, rev 1853, 1859)

Totentanz means 'Dance of Death' and was inspired by a fresco, *The Triumph of Death*, in the Campo Santo in Pisa. The work is a single-movement fantasy for piano and orchestra using, as one of its themes, the Dies Irae ("Day of Wrath"). Turn up the sound sytem full volume – there are spectacular flights of virtuosity from the piano and the whole work exudes terror and diabolism.

Transcriptions and arrangements for piano

The range of composers whose works Liszt adapted is quite remarkable, a tribute to an extraordinary catholic knowledge and taste - everything from Bach organ preludes and fugues and a Handel Sarabande and Chaconne to works by Rossini, Saint-Saëns, Tchaikovsky and dozens of others.

PIANO SONATA
(1853)
A work of huge ambition and massive scale

In any discussion of piano music, the Liszt Sonata, as it's known, looms large, the crowning glory of his achievements as a writer for the piano and one of the 19th century's musical monuments. It lasts about half an hour and is full of ground-breaking ideas: it expands the customary form of the sonata (three or four contrasted movements with appropriate development sections); instead, Liszt builds a tightly-knit structure using five themes or motifs to unify one huge single movement while nevertheless retaining the outward vestiges of the traditional sonata. The concluding section, a *Prestissimo*, recalls all the basic themes. The American critic James Gibbons Huneker thought, "Nothing more exciting is there in the literature of the piano."

61

The recording

ARNALDO COHEN

⊙ BIS BIS-CD1253 + ➡

Arnaldo Cohen's playing blazes with the risk-taking, spontaneity and urgency of a live concert. The Liszt Sonata, Cohen's second recording, mingles narrative and textual clarity with a musical maturity and heady virtuosity in the Richter class. This is a performance to stand alongside the very greatest – an example of towering pianism.

If you like this, try: Liszt's 12 Etudes d'exécution transcendante • Scriabin's Piano Sonata No 9, "Black Mass" • Dukas's Piano Sonata • Schubert/Liszt Wanderer Fantasy

PIANO CONCERTOS
(1835-1861)

Two siblings: very different but each with considerable charm

You could call the Liszt No 1 the brilliant-spectacular concerto, while No 2 is the poetic-spiritual one. In No 1, instead of having three or four separate musically unconnected movements (as in the traditional concerto), Liszt linked his four together by returning to themes he'd used earlier in the concerto as a unifying element. It's still one of the most played of all piano concertos. Liszt developed the one-movement idea with his Second Concerto, but instead of linking three or four movements into one, he wrote in a series of highly-contrasted sections using fewer themes but harking back to them in various guises throughout the work. It's in a more pensive, less showy vein than No 1, though it's not without its flashy moments. Liszt called it a "concerto symphonique" to underline the importance of the orchestral contribution and its relationship to the piano.

The recording

**ELDAR NEBOLSIN
ROYAL LIVERPOOL PHILHARMONIC
ORCHESTRA / VASILY PETRENKO**

⊙ Naxos 8.570517 + ⊟

Not only can the performances hold their own with the very best but the individual concertos compare with those by the likes of Katchen and Richter. Nebolsin, winner of the first Sviatoslav Richter International Piano Competition in 2005, is a virtuoso of power and poetry. While allowing the music to breathe, he plays in long paragraphs without, as it were, having to come up for air. Try the

scintillating final pages of the First Concerto in which Petrenko, always an alert partner, catches the ball and runs with it. Recorded sound is exemplary. At super-budget price, the disc is a real bargain.

If you like this, try: Liszt's Piano Sonata • Tchaikovsky's Piano Concerto No 1 • Saint-Saëns's Piano Concerto No 2 • Chopin's Piano Concerto No 2 • Liszt's Totentanz

GUSTAV MAHLER

Born Kaliste 1860 **Died** Vienna 1911

Mahler is the last great Romantic symphonist, music conceived on the grandest scale and employing elaborate forces. He wanted to express his view of the human condition, to set down his lofty ideals about Life, Death and the Universe. "My symphonies represent the contents of my entire life."

Mahler's tragic childhood stalked him for the whole of his life. The young Mahler frequently witnessed the brutality meted out to his long-suffering mother by an ambitious father, the owner of a small brandy distillery. Of his 12 siblings, five died in infancy of diphtheria, one brother died aged 12, another was a simpleton in his youth and a forger in his adult life, yet another committed suicide, his oldest sister died of a brain tumor and another fantasised that she was dying.

When he was six, Mahler discovered a piano in the attic of his grandmother's house. Four years later he gave his first solo piano recital and at the age of 15 he enrolled at the Vienna Conservatoire. It was here that he discovered a talent for conducting. After a succession of ever more important posts he took over the Royal Opera House in Budapest from 1886 to 1888, then on to Hamburg before finally winning in 1897 the position he yearned for: artistic director of the Vienna Opera and soon after of the Vienna Philharmonic. He remained at the opera for ten years and in that decade raised its fortunes to a height which some say has never been equalled since.

In 1901 he married Alma Schindler, step-daughter of the avant-garde Viennese artist Carl Moll. She was beautiful, well-read and a composer in her own right but Mahler demanded that she give up her composing and be totally subservient to his wishes.

The first five years of marriage saw Mahler at the height of his powers and at his happiest. He continued to compose as he had during the previous decade

in the one form to which he aspired and (to his austere way of thinking) in the highest form of musical expression – the orchestral symphony.

By 1906 he had completed the Fifth, Sixth and Seventh Symphonies, each one vaster in scale than its predecessor, each one greeted with hostility, misunderstandings and vituperation. Mahler was impervious to all around him, convinced that "my time will come".

Then in 1907 personal tragedy hit him. One of his little daughters died from scarlet fever. Mahler went insane with grief. In 1903 he had composed a set of songs entitled *Kindertotenlieder* – "Songs on the Death of Children". Forever after he carried around with him the guilt that he had been responsible in part for his child's death, guilt for tempting fate. In the same year (1907) that he decided to leave Vienna he was told he had a serious heart condition. The remaining four years of his life were focused on America. He first went to the Metropolitan Opera for two unhappy seasons, then in 1909 took over the conductorship of the New York Philharmonic. The audience disliked him and the orchestra loathed him. The feeling was entirely mutual.

In September 1910 he was in Munich to conduct the premiere of his mammoth Eighth Symphony, which met with overwhelming success, one of the few triumphs he ever witnessed as a composer. He returned to New York in late 1910 but early the next year a severe blood infection led to his premature death at the age of 50 in a Vienna nursing home.

63

SYMPHONY NO 1
(1888 rev 1893 & 1896)

Mahler's entry into the world of the symphony sings with nature

Mahler's First Symphony was finished in 1888 when he was 28 (he revised it twice afterwards). He described it as "the sound of Nature" – and it is full of the countryside, ingratiating dance melodies and rhythms. Despite his lifelong aversion to attaching titles and programmatic interpretations to his work, he endowed this symphony with precise labels, breaking it into two parts, the first "Days of Youth", the second "Commedia umana" with each of the four (originally five) movements also given descriptive titles. Later he gave the whole work the title "Titan", after the novel of the same name by the German poet Jean Paul, which he greatly admired at the time (he dropped the subtitle later).

The recording

BAVARIAN RADIO SYMPHONY ORCHESTRA / RAFAEL KUBELÍK
⊙ DG 449 735-2GOR + ⏵

Rafael Kubelík is essentially a poetic conductor and he gets more poetry out of this symphony than almost any other conductor who has recorded it. Notwithstanding a fondness for generally brisk tempos in Mahler, Kubelík is never afraid of rubato here, above all in his very personally inflected account of the slow movement. This remains a delight. The orchestral contribution is very good, even if absolute precision isn't guaranteed.

TULLY POTTER COLLECTION

If you like this, try: Mahler's Des Knaben Wunderhorn • Bruckner's Fourth Symphony • Hans Rott's Symphony • Suk's Asrael Symphony • Tchaikovsky's Symphony No 1

MAHLER ESSENTIALS

Symphony No 2, 'Resurrection' (1886 rev.1896)

It calls for gargantuan forces – a pipe organ, church bells, off-stage horns, trumpets and percussion, a soprano, contralto and chorus. If you were to subject the work to a programmatic interpretation you could say that the first movement is about death, the second about youthful optimism, the third about life's vulgarities and the fourth about spiritual life; the last movement is Judgement Day. In other words, the symphony is an allegory on the life of man.

Symphony No 4 (1900)

Perhaps the most accessible of the nine for Mahler beginners, this most joyous of all his symphonies is also the shortest, culminating in a fourth movement with a soprano singing the text of an old Bavarian folk-song from Mahler's own song cycle *Des Knaben Wunderhorn*. Bruno Walter, the great conductor and disciple of Mahler, thought that "a devout piety dreams its dream of heaven".

Das Lied von der Erde (1909)

"The Song of the Earth" is considered by many to be Mahler's most beautiful and most personal work. He began but never completed a Tenth Symphony (it was left for others to provide its conjectural end), but Mahler referred to this work as "a symphony". Thus, although you'll never find it numbered as such, this can be regarded as Mahler's real Tenth. (Fate had a habit of terminating composers' lives after their ninth symphonies – Beethoven, Bruckner and Dvořák – and the superstitious Mahler was determined to outwit Fate.) He uses poems by Chinese writers which examine the nature of human life as a transient stage in a constant earth-renewing process.

SYMPHONY NO 5
(1902)
The most popular of Mahler's symphonies

Lasting over an hour and a quarter, Mahler's Fifth has five movements beginning, unusally, with a funeral march. Mahler insisted that "not a single note points to the influence of extra-musical thoughts or emotions upon the composition of the Fifth", yet it seems to tell a story of passionate intensity. The *Adagietto*, the Symphony's fourth movement, is most probably a gently flowing love song but is more often seen as an outpouring of grief and yearning made famous by its effective use in Visconti's film of Thomas Mann's novel *Death in Venice* (a rouged Dirk Bogarde sitting in a deckchair pining for a blonde Adonis) and also by generations of conductors drawing it out to a virtual standstill.

65

The recording

NEW PHILHARMONIA ORCHESTRA / SIR JOHN BARBIROLLI

⊙ EMI 566910-2 + ⮕

Sir John Barbirolli's Fifth occupies a special place in everybody's affections: a performance so big in spirit and warm of heart as to silence any rational discussion of its shortcomings. Some may have problems with one or two of his sturdier tempos. He doesn't make the orchestra's life easy in the treacherous second movement, while the exultant finale, though suitably bracing, arguably needs more of a spring in its heels. But against all this, one must weigh a wonderful unity and strength of purpose.

If you like this, try: Mahler's Symphony No 9 • Sibelius's Symphony No 6 • Tchaikovsky's Symphony No 4 • Shostakovich's Symphony No 5 • Prokofiev's Symphony No 6

FELIX MENDELSSOHN

Born Hamburg 1809 **Died** Leipzig 1847

Mendelssohn is one of the "Sunshine Composers" who, like Rossini and Saint-Saëns, wrote effortless, life-enhancing, optimistic music. "Felix" is the Latin for "happy" an auspicious choice for it reflects the character of the man and his music.

Mendelssohn came from a wealthy and cultured Jewish family. By the time he was nine, he was a good enough pianist to appear in public; at 10 he joined the Singakademie in Berlin; by the age of 12 he had composed several symphonies, two operas and other works. Seeing that his son's future was to be in music and how many paths were closed to Jews in the musical world, Mendelssohn's father decided to convert from the Jewish faith to Protestantism. Later, the composer and his wife followed suit, adding "Bartholdy" to their name to distinguish them from other Mendelssohns who were still Jewish.

The Mendelssohn house was always filled with the distinguished and influential. He was taken by his teacher to Weimar and introduced to Goethe. The 70-year-old writer and the 12-year-old prodigy became firm friends. All who met the young Mendelssohn and heard him play left incredulous. Here, without a doubt, was a second Mozart. In fact, by the time he was 16 Mendelssohn was composing music of far greater maturity than that which Mozart had written at a similar age: the overture to *A Midsummer Night's Dream* and his Octet are extraordinarily assured and original. He was only 20 when he conducted a performance of Bach's *St Mathew Passion* at the Berlin Singakademie, an event which, more than any other, propelled a general revival of interest in Bach's music. Not long after, he made the first of 10 visits to England, feted as a

celebrity and conducting the premiere of his C minor Symphony before travelling to Scotland.

After an unhappy spell conducting in Düsseldorf, he was made musical director of the famous Leipzig Gewandhaus Orchestra. During 1835 and the next five years, Mendelssohn turned the orchestra into the finest in the world. In 1837 he married the 17-year-old daughter of a French Protestant clergyman and, as you'd expect, enjoyed an idyllically happy life together with their five children. Six years later he founded the Leipzig Conservatory. Now working at a furious pace – conducting, teaching, composing, giving concerts – his health began to suffer. Pains in the head and abnormal fatigue kept recurring. He was in Birmingham for the premiere of his oratorio *Elijah* in August 1846 (one of the greatest receptions of his career) before returning to Leipzig, followed by a further visit to England in the spring of 1847 where he played for Queen Victoria, his long-time and fervent admirer. In May, news reached him that his beloved sister Fanny had died suddenly. The loss had a devastating effect on Mendelssohn. Hearing of her death, he became unconscious, rupturing a blood vessel in the head. He only ever partly recovered. All the life went out of him, he began suffering terrible depressions and agonising pain. Less than six months later, he too was dead. He was 38. There were memorial services held in most of the principal cities in Germany as well as in London, Manchester, Birmingham and Paris.

67

VIOLIN CONCERTO
(1845)
Still the most popular violin concerto of them all

The Mendelssohn Violin Concerto, as it's universally referred to (though he did compose one other) came about as the result of his long friendship with the composer and celebrated violinist Ferdinand David (1810-73). It was written over a period of five years, with many consultations between the two, and it was not until March 1845 in Leipzig that it received its first performance – David the soloist, Niels Gade, the Danish composer, on the podium (Mendelssohn was having an enforced rest in Frankfurt). Its popularity with violinists and audiences has not diminished since that day.

If you like this, try: Mendelssohn's Concerto for Violin, Piano and Strings • Mendelssohn's piano concertos • Beethoven's Violin Concerto • Dvořák's Violin Concerto

The recording

**NIGEL KENNEDY
ENGLISH CHAMBER
ORCHESTRA / JEFFREY TATE**
⊙ EMI 749663-2 + ⯮

Kennedy's view of the Mendelssohn has a positive, masculine quality established at the very start. He may at first seem a little fierce, but fantasy goes with firm control and the transition into the second subject on a descending arpeggio (marked *tranquillo*) is radiantly beautiful. He is unerringly helped by Jeffrey Tate's sympathetic support.

SYMPHONY NO 4
"Italian" (1833)
An ageless hymn to vitality and the poetry of Italy

Here is Mendelssohn's impression of Italy. He visited the country after his trip to Britain in 1829 and, still only 22, wrote this ebullient, carefree response. Listen to the opening of the first movement – you can taste the excitement Mendelssohn must have felt at the prospect before him. The slow movement has been referred to as a "pilgrim's march" but, though he witnessed the coronation of Pope Gregory XVI while in Rome, there's no evidence to confirm that this was what Mendelssohn intended. The finale, the only genuine Italian thing about the symphony, is a *saltarello*, a vigorous Italian peasant dance.

If you like this, try: Mendelssohn's Symphony No 1 • Mendelssohn's string symphonies • Schumann's Symphony No 1 • Brahms's Symphony No 3

The recording

**LONDON SYMPHONY
ORCHESTRA / CLAUDIO
ABBADO**
⊙ DG 427 810-2GDC + ⯮

Abbado imparts a winning sense of structural direction and emotional abandon to these works. The myth of Mendelssohn the simple prodigy is satisfyingly exploded. Abbado's Mendelssohn recordings with the London Symphony Orchestra, of which he was music director, remain a richly rewarding legacy.

MENDELSSOHN ESSENTIALS

A Midsummer Night's Dream – incidental music (1826 and 1842)

The famous Overture, written when Mendelssohn was 17, is a miracle for the work of a boy; here, already, is his mature style with its "light, aerial, airy" reaches. Few could spot the join between this and the remaining parts of the incidental music written at the request of the King of Prussia 16 years later. The most frequently heard sections are the Scherzo and the Wedding March; the latter has accompanied countless happy couples down the aisle.

The Hebrides Overture (Fingal's Cave) (1830)

In the spring of 1829 Mendelssohn made his first visit to Britain and journeyed up to Scotland. He made a trip to Staffa, off the Isle of Mull, and saw the celebrated Fingal's Cave. The Overture is a terrific "sea piece" – you can just see the waves rolling into the cliffs round Staffa – which gets its double title from the fact that Mendelssohn scribbled "Fingal's Cave" on the front of the original score, while the orchestral parts were marked "The Hebrides".

Elijah (1846)

Mendelssohn had the idea of writing a choral work about the prophet Elijah in 1836, soon after he had completed the writing of his first oratorio St Paul. But it was not until 1845, when the Birmingham Music Festival invited him to compose a work for the 1846 festival, that he set to work on the project. The first performance, with the composer conducting, was an overwhelming success and, for more than a century, when it came to great oratorios, Elijah was second in popularity only to Handel's Messiah.

HANYA CHLALA/ARENAPAL

OCTET
(1825)

In four movements, the Octet is one of the marvels of all chamber music

The Mendelssohn family lived in a large house on the outskirts of Berlin and on Sunday mornings held concerts – an excellent training ground for the young composer. Here Mendelssohn played and absorbed the chamber works of the great composers and was able to hear his own music played and criticised by fine musicians. By the age of 12 he was an experienced writer for stringed instruments. Even so, the Octet of 1825 is an amazing achievement. Not even those other child prodigies Mozart or Schubert produced anything of this maturity at a comparable age, added to which it was the first truly integrated work for eight string players.

69

The recording

NASH ENSEMBLE

⊙ Wigmore Hall Live WHLIVE00001 + ⇥
This is a recording from a concert given in March 2005; a very good recording, too, combining intimacy with the warm ambience familiar to Wigmore Hall concertgoers. The outer movements of the Mendelssohn have plenty of fire and spirit. The climax of the first movement's development section is grand and intense, with the  following *pianissimo* full of romantic mystery and suspense. Throughout

the performance, the ensemble's sheer joy of playing together is a delight to hear. There's no doubting the genuine enthusiasm of the applause at the end.

If you like this, try: Mendelssohn's String Quartet, Op 80 • Schubert's Octet • Brahms's string sextets • Tchaikovsky's Souvenirs de Florence • Poulenc's Sextet

TURANGALÎLA-SYMPHONIE
(1881-85)
A work that defies definition

Rhythm was a particular pre-occupation of Messiaen demonstrated no more vividly than in this massive 10-movement "apotheosis of rhythm", commissioned by the Koussevitzky Foundation and conducted by Leonard Bernstein at its premiere in 1949. The word "Turangalîla" is a word derived from the Sanskrit, "turanga" meaning "time" and "lîla" meaning "love". Though a vastly complicated work which requires many hearings to absorb, the symphony can be an overwhelming experience for first-time listeners, who usually remark on the inclusion in the score of the vast array of percussion instruments on show and the other-worldly sound of the onde martenot, an electronic keyboard invented in 1928 by one Maurice Martenot.

70

A complex and original thinker, Messiaen (1908-92) delighted in the use of elaborate rhythmic and exotic harmonic ideas.

Probably the only classical composer to have a mountain named after him (Mount Messiaen, Utah, 1978), Messiaen is among the most strikingly individual of 20th-century composers. He entered the Paris Conservatoire at the age of 11, specialising in organ, improvisation and composition. When he graduated in 1930, he not only became organist at L'Eglise de la Trinité in Paris but also began a distinguished teaching career and co-founded a group called "La Jeune France", which had the express intention of promoting modern French music.

He joined the French army at the outbreak of the Second World War but was taken prisoner and spent two years in a German prison camp. Here he composed his *Quatuor pour le fin du temps*. Repatriated in 1942, he resumed his post at la Trinité and was appointed to the faculty of the Paris Conservatoire. From then, his career as France's leading living composer developed apace and by the early 1950s he had an international standing. Three generations of young composers studied with him.

Perhaps the most remarkable area of his huge breadth of knowledge was as an ornithologist. He catalogued the songs of every known French bird and also those of Africa, India and South America. His *Oiseaux exotique*, *Catalogue des oiseaux* and *Réveil des oiseaux* are just some of the intricate works which use bird song as their inspiration. Above all was Messiaen's devotion to the Roman Catholic faith. The mystic and celebratory elements are at the root of all his music: the celebration of God's love for human beings and the human soul's yearning for God.

The recording

PIERRE-LAURENT AIMARD; DOMINIQUE KIM; BERLIN PHILHARMONIC / KENT NAGANO

⊙ Teldec 8573 82043-2 + ⤷

Turangalîla is a difficult score, and to record it live is risky. Whether despite or because of that risk this is a splendidly exciting performance; more surprisingly it's also for the most part a very accurate and detailed one. The soloists are admirable; the extremes of the piano part, in particular, are just what Aimard is good at.

If you like this, try: Messiaen's L'Ascension • Wagner's Tristan und Isolde • Szymanowski's Symphony No 4 • Schoenberg's Gurrelieder • Bartók's Bluebeard's Castle

MONTEVERDI

Monteverdi (1567-1643) is one of the great original minds of music, the first great writer of operas and a technical innovator. In Monteverdi you find the culmination of the Renaissance and the door swinging wide open to reveal the new Baroque period – and beyond.

Monteverdi's life falls into two distinct sections. The first part began in Cremona where he studied with the maestro di cappella at the Cathedral. He had his first compositions published when only 15. A stroke of good luck in 1592 led him to a position in the court of Vincenzo I, Duke of Mantua, as a viol player and singer. His patron was in the habit of taking a musical retinue wherever he went, whether it was to Hungary to fight a war or to Flanders to take a water-cure for gout. Monteverdi was thus able to hear current musical trends elsewhere on the continent. He was made head of the musical household, he married one of the court singers, he was able to write what music he wanted and the Duke paid for its publication. Perfect. Then it all went wrong.

His wife died in 1607 and he suffered a nervous breakdown; Vincenzo I died to be succeeded by Francesco Gonzaga who summarily dismissed him. A fire destroyed the manuscripts of 12 operas he had written and, when he was appointed to become head of music at St Mark's in Venice in 1613 he was set upon by highwaymen on his way there and robbed of everything he owned. From the secular works of the first part of his life he concentrated mainly on religious music.

He remained in Venice for the rest of his life. Even after he took holy orders in 1632, Monteverdi continued to produce both secular and sacred music, seemingly more content in the service of God than the Venetian court, but the opening of the first opera house in Venice in 1637 inspired him, in old age, to write a remarkable five more operas.

VESPERS
(1610)
Monteverdi's outstanding achievement in sacred music

Shortly before the composition of *Vespro della Beata Vergine* (Vespers of the Blessed Virgin), to give this exalted work its formal title, Monteverdi had suffered the loss of both his wife (1607) and his only child (1608), a promising young singer. This is Monteverdi's outstanding achievement in sacred music, a richly-scored setting of the service of Vespers for soloists, choir and orchestra written in the new operatic style of the time and quite different to the church style of, say, Palestrina. The variety of ways in which he uses the instrumental and vocal forces sets it apart from those of his contemporaries – the duet "Two Seraphims", for example, is an operatic duet (or is it a duel) for two angels. The "Magnificat" and "Sancta Maria" sections are often heard independently. The work is dedicated to Pope Paul V.

The recording

MONTEVERDI CHOIR / JOHN ELIOT GARDINER

⊙ Archiv 429 565-2AH2 + ▷

This large-scale live recording of Monteverdi's magisterial masterpiece (Gardiner's second – the first, on Decca, drew on some of the finest English singers of its day, and is also well worth hearing) was made in Venice's St Mark's Basilica.

It captures the drama as well as the ceremonial aspect of the work, despite

sometimes cloudy recorded sound. Also available on DVD.

If you like this, try: Monteverdi's Madrigals • Monteverdi's L'Orfeo • Monteverdi's Coronation of Poppea • Buxtehude's Sacred Cantatas • Vivaldi's Gloria • Rachmaninov's Vespers

Sir Charles Mackerras
Conductor
A great musician whose
Mozart is the stuff of
modern legend (page 74)

WOLFGANG AMADEUS MOZART

Born Salzburg 1756 **Died** Vienna 1791

Mozart was arguably the most naturally gifted musician in history, but he also worked assiduously to become far and away the greatest composer, pianist, violinist and conductor of his day – it was not just in one area of music that he was supreme, but in all fields.

Both Wolfgang and his sister Anna Maria were keyboard prodigies, and their ambitious father Leopold, a composer and violinist in the service of the Prince Archbishop of Salzburg, set about exploiting their gifts to the full.

In 1762, the three set off for a long tour of Germany, Belgium, Paris, London (1764-65) and Holland. By the time he arrived back in Salzburg, Mozart had composed his first three symphonies, plus some 30 other works and arrangements. In 1768 he wrote his first stage work, the following year travelling to Italy with his father where they stayed for two years. Here he took lessons from Martini and is said to have copied down Allegri's *Miserere* from memory. This was followed by a period in Salzburg in which he composed his first important works, including the five violin concertos. After another tour to Paris, he returned to Salzburg where he spent the next two years composing in the service of the Archbishop. *Idomeneo* (1780), his first important opera, was among the commissions he received (from the Elector of Bavaria) but frustrated by the stultifying demands of his employer, Mozart resigned from the Archbishop's service.

Mozart decided to make Vienna his home, a move which marks the beginning of his golden years as a mature composer. He married Constanze Weber in August 1782, a few days after the first performance of his opera *Die Entführung aus dem Serail*. A string of fine works now appeared (the *Haffner* and *Linz* symphonies, a set of six string quartets dedicated to Haydn – the two had become close friends – as well as *The Marriage of Figaro* in 1786). The last nine years of Mozart's life find him juggling a precarious financial position whilst pouring out masterpieces in every genre. At last, in November 1787, he secured an appointment as Kammermusicus in Vienna, a change in his financial fortunes that must have softened the blow of his father's death earlier in the year, the same year that saw the appearance of *Don Giovanni*, his second operatic masterpiece. The succession of enduring works he completed in the final four years is quite staggering, among them *Eine kleine Nachtmusik*, the exquisite Clarinet Quintet, three highly contrasted symphonies (No 39 in E flat, No 40 in G minor and No 41 in C , *Jupiter*), the opera *Così fan tutte*, two piano sonatas, three string quartets and much else besides.

Though offered the post of Kapellmeister in Berlin and the opportunity to establish himself in London, Mozart remained in Vienna. In 1791 came the Clarinet Concerto and Piano Concerto No 27 in B flat, *The Magic Flute* and the Requiem – any one of which would have ensured a composer's immortality. But by now Mozart's health began to fail dramatically. He did not live long enough to complete his Requiem before he died horribly, from a number of bodily failures, a few weeks before his 36th birthday.

SYMPHONY NO 41 "JUPITER" (1788)
The crowning glory of the 18th century symphony

Without any formal introduction, Mozart launches into one of the most lyrical openings of any symphony, a work of which Schubert said: "You can hear the angels singing in it". The whole symphony has a quiet character that suggests the end of summer and the first shades of autumn. No one seems sure how the *Jupiter* acquired its nickname. Some think it arose in England in the 1820s due to the composer and publisher Johann Baptist Cramer who was impressed by the God-like perfection of the work. This, his final symphony, is the crowning glory of any work in this form written in the 18th century.

If you like this, try: Mozart's Symphonies Nos 39 & 40 • Mozart's "Haffner" Serenade • Haydn's "London" Symphonies • Beethoven's Symphonies Nos 1 & 2

PIANO CONCERTOS NO 21, 23 & 24 (1785 & 1786)
Works that seem to glimpse into Mozart's soul with delight

For the most part, Mozart's 27 piano concertos are sunny and optimistic. No 21 (K467), right from the opening bars, is turbulent and angry in mood. It was the first he wrote in a minor key and its drama and passion was a musical signpost to the future. A year later (March 1786), Mozart penned two piano concertos simultaneously, in contrasting moods. The A major (K488) has a suave, welcoming theme which introduces the most lyrical of all his piano concertos. Its companion (No 24 in C minor, K491) is, by general consent, one of the greatest piano concertos ever written.

If you like this, try: Mozart's Quintet for Piano and Wind Instruments • Beethoven's Piano Concertos Nos 1 & 2 • Chopin's Piano Concerto No 1 • Schubert's Impromptus

MOZART ESSENTIALS

Horn Concerto No 4 in E flat (1786)

Ignaz Leutgeb, who was already 50 when Mozart produced these concertos, must have been a very able player to negotiate the many demanding passages Mozart wrote for the French horn of his time. Modern horns make the solo part easier to play but, like all Mozart, is never easy to play well. Though many fine versions have appeared subsequently, the classic recordings were made in 1953 by the English virtuoso Dennis Brain. No 4 has one of the composer's best-known movements (the final Rondo).

Serenade No 10 in B flat for 13 wind instruments (1781-84)

His serenades, divertimenti and other chamber works may have been written for entertainment purposes, but Mozart invested in the music his innermost feelings and all the gifts at his disposal. The extraordinary Serenade for 13 wind instruments is like a symphony in its structure except that it's longer than any of Mozart's symphonies (it lasts about 50 minutes) and is in seven movements. The score requests a pair each of oboes, clarinets, basset-horns and bassoons, plus four horns and a contra-bassoon.

The Magic Flute (1791)

Beethoven considered thisopera to be Mozart's greatest work and the distinguished critic Sir Neville Cardus wote, "The opera … is the only one in existence that might conceivably have been composed by God." *The Magic Flute* works on many levels – as a fairy tale, an allegory, a pantomime or a glorification of freemasonry (Mozart and his librettist Schikaneder were Masons). After its premiere, its popularity was such that it was performed more than 100 times in the first year alone – not that Mozart knew, for little over two months after the opening night he was dead.

CAMI

CLARINET CONCERTO
(1791)
The work that introduced the human voice into the symphony

The Clarinet Concerto was written in the last few months of Mozart's life. It is said that he started work on it on September 28, 1791 and completed it on October 7 – the same week that he was conducting the first performances of *The Magic Flute*! Like the Clarinet Quintet in the same key, the Concerto was written for Mozart's friend the celebrated virtuoso Anton Stadler (1753-1812). Mozart wrote for the very limit of the contemporary instrument's potential – it had only six keys whereas the modern clarinet has nearly 20. The two outer movements are lively *allegro*s but the heart of the work is the central *Adagio*, surely one of the most beautiful slow movements in music.

75

The recording

**THEA KING
ENGLISH CHAMBER ORCHESTRA /
JEFFREY TATE**

⊙ Hyperion CDA66199 + ⮫

Coupled with the equally lovely Clarinet Quintet (with the Gabrieli Quartet), this is a delightful performance of Mozart's late Clarinet Concerto. Its melodic freedom is wonderfully conveyed by Thea King's fluid, poetic playing, and Jeffrey Tate and the ECO are the perfect partners in Mozart: attentive, imaginative and always sprightly.

If you like this, try: Mozart's Clarinet Quintet • Spohr's Clarinet Concerto • Stanford's Clarinet Concerto • Finzi's Clarinet Concerto • Brahms's Clarinet Quintet

REQUIEM
(1791)
The work Haydn requested for his own Requiem Mass

Mozart was visited by a tall, thin stranger who delivered an anonymous letter requesting a Requiem to be written in the shortest possible time for an anonymous patron. Mozart, already suffering from the illnesses that were to prove fatal, became convinced that a messenger from another world had invited him to write his own requiem. Its composition did indeed prove to be a race with death. (The anonymous stranger proved to be the steward of Count Franz von Walsegg, who wanted a requiem in memory of his late wife, but Mozart never learned this.) The composer managed to finish 12 of the Requiem's 15 sections before he died, but left detailed instructions for its completion by his pupil Süssmayr. It is an extraordinary work ranging from despair and terror to exaltation and elegiac peace.

76

The recording

CHRISTINE SCHÄFER; BERNARDA FINK; KURT STREIT; GERALD FINLEY; ARNOLD SCHOENBERG CHOIR; CONCENTUS MUSICIUS WIEN / NIKOLAUS HARNONCOURT
⊙ DHM 82876 58705-2 + ⮕
This isn't a recording of the Requiem that comforts and stirs in the expected ways: instead a curious and enigmatic undertow of human vulnerability emerges, presenting Mozart's valedictory essay in a striking new light. Glorious solo singing and thrilling choral work.

SONY CLASSICAL

If you like this, try: Mozart's C minor Mass • Haydn's The Creation • Beethoven's Mass in C • Beethoven's Missa solemnis • Schubert's Mass No 6 in E flat, D960

THE MARRIAGE OF FIGARO
(1786)

Could this be the most perfect opera ever written?

Figaro is Mozart's comic masterpiece, one of the most popular and frequently performed of all operas. The opening night (May 1, 1786 in Vienna) ran twice as long as planned because everything was encored. The complicated plot is based on the second of three plays by Beaumarchais (Rossini's opera *The Barber of Seville* is based on the first) featuring the rascally Figaro and the amorous exploits of Count and Countess Almaviva, and Cherubino and Susanna, their page and maid. The popular Overture is a sparkling mood-setter, while the many vocal highlights include Cherubino's "Non so più" ("I know not what I am") and "Voi che sapete" ("You who understand"), Figaro's "Non più andrai" ("No more games") and the Countess's two exquisite arias "Porgi amor" ("Grant O love") and "Dove sono" ("I remember days long departed").

77

The recording

LORENZO REGAZZO; PATRIZIA CIOFI; SIMON KEENLYSIDE; VÉRONIQUE GENS; ANGELIKA KIRCHSCHLAGER; CONCERTO KÖLN / RENÉ JACOBS

⊙ Harmonia Mundi HMC90 1818/20

The cast is excellent. Véronique Gens offers a beautifully natural, shapely "Porgi amor" and a passionate and spirited "Dove sono". The laughter in Patrizia Ciofi's voice is delightful when she's dressing up Cherubino. Then there's Angelika Kirschlager's Cherubino, alive and urgent in "Non so più". Lorenzo Regazzo offers a strong Figaro, with a wide range of voice – angry and determined in "Se vuol ballare", nicely rhythmic with some softer colours in "Non più andrai", and pain and bitterness in "Aprite'". The Count of Simon Keenlyside is powerful, menacing, lean and dark in tone.

If you like this, try: Mozart's The Magic Flute • Mozart's Così fan tutte • Rossini's The Barber of Seville • Cimarosa's Susanna's Secret • Richard Strauss's Der Rosenkavalier

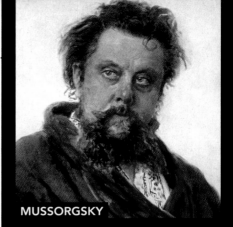

MUSSORGSKY

PICTURES AT AN EXHIBITION
(1874)
Real painting in music

In 1873 the Russian painter and architect Vladimir Hartmann died. He had been a close friend of Mussorgsky and the critic Vladimir Stasov, inspired by Mussorgsky, organised an exhibition of Hartmann's paintings and sketches in St Petersburg. Mussorgsky took his personal tribute a step further by writing the equivalent of a musical tour of the gallery with pianistic depictions of some of the works on show. *Pictures at an Exhibition* illustrates 11 pictures in 10 separate movements. Linking them is a recurring theme representing, as Mussorgsky explained, "the composer… walking idly through the gallery, pausing occasionally to observe a picture and think sadly of his friend". The suite is one of the most important pieces of Russian piano music but is more familiar today in Ravel's orchestration.

78

Mussorgsky wanted to express the Russian people in music. "When I sleep I see them, when I eat I think of them, when I drink – I can visualise them."

Mussorgsky (1839-81) came from wealthy, land-owning aristocracy. His musical talent was nurtured by his mother. In 1856 he took a military commission. The following year he was introduced to the composers Balakirev and Cui and he also became friendly with the critic Stasov, the main champion of Russian national music. Already a heavy drinker, Mussorgsky abandoned his military career forthwith.

In 1861, when the serfs were emancipated, his family went bankrupt, forcing him into paid work as a clerk in the Ministry of Communications. During the next four years he composed continuously, though his lack of a formal musical education led him to abandon most of the works he began. He resigned from his job in 1865. Two years later, Stasov defined the "mighty handful of Russian musicians", known today as "The Mighty Handful": Mussorgsky, Balakirev, Borodin, Cui and Rimsky-Korsakov.

By this time, Mussorgsky was living in abject poverty. In 1869 he entered government service again. Simultaneously he worked on his great opera *Boris Godunov*, which eventually saw the light of day in St Petersburg in 1874. Its success was tempered by strong criticism by Mussorgsky's fellow musicians and this upset him greatly. Now a dipsomaniac, Mussorgsky began a second opera *Khovanshchina* (left incomplete at his death) but his concentration and lifestyle had disintegrated and he suffered from delirium tremens and epileptic fits. He died following one such fit just a week after his 42nd birthday.

The recording

PHILHARMONIA ORCHESTRA / VLADIMIR ASHKENAZY & VLADIMIR ASHKENAZY

⊙ Decca 475 7717DOR + ⊟→

This interesting disc coupled the original piano score with Vladimir Ashkenazy's own orchestration – and having the same musician as pianist and conductor adds to the fascination. Ashkenazy clearly loves this work and brings his formidable pianism to bear on the Mussorgsky original, and with the Philharmonia on top form, he provides an intriguing commentary on the score in his own orchestration.

If you like this, try: Balakirev's Islamey • Tchaikovsky's The Seasons • Scriabin's piano sonatas • Borodin's Symphony No 2 • Rachmaninov's Corelli Variations

NIELSEN

Anyone seeking a gentle introduction to 20th-century music could do worse than listen to the six symphonies by this remarkable composer, Denmark's most important and at last an acknowledged master.

In his charming autobiography, *My Childhood*, Nielsen (1865-1931) tells of his bucolic early life on the peasant island community of Fünen in eastern Denmark (also the birthplace of Hans Christian Andersen) where his father was an itinerant labourer and keen amateur fiddle player. The Danish soil and character (though not so much its folk music) pervades all his work; there's an attractive, unsentimental directness about it and, though it has its bleak moments, a life-affirming spirit abounds in music of clear-cut colours and structures.

After rudimentary lessons from his father, at the age of 14 he joined the military band in Odense as a trombonist, though his first job had been as a shepherd. After studying at the Royal Conservatory in Copenhagen, where one of his teachers was Niels Gade, the founding father of the Scandinavian school of composition and friend of Schumann and Mendelssohn, in 1889 Nielsen was employed as a violinist in the Royal Theatre Orchestra. On and off, he retained his connection with this and the Royal Opera Orchestra, either playing or conducting, until 1914.

Meanwhile, he had made something of a name for himself with his attractive Suite for Strings (1888). In 1890 a scholarship took him to Germany. During this trip, he met and married (within eight weeks) a gifted and strong-willed sculptress, Anna Marie Brodersen (1863-1945), with whom he had three children. It proved to be a tempestuous relationship with long periods spent apart, threats of divorce and at least one extra-marital affair (with the children's governess), though they remained together until Nielsen's death.

SYMPHONY NO 4
"Inextinguishable" (1914-16)

A symphony that taps into man's elemental will to live

In each symphony he wrote, Nielsen tried out something new. No 1, for instance, begins in one key and ends in another; No 2, inspired by a woodcut Nielsen spotted in a country pub, is subtitled "The Four Temperaments" and depicts these (anger, phlegmatism, melancholy and optimism) in successive movements. No 4, "The Inextinguishable", was written mid-war and alternates between bombastic fury and reflective optimism. It's a work of high drama that culminates in a kind of musical duel between two sets of timpani ranged either side of the orchestra. The title refers not to the symphony but rather to man's inextinguishable life-force, the elemental will to live. It's approachable but also thrilling in its exploration of a unique musical language.

79

The recording

SAN FRANCISCO SYMPHONY ORCHESTRA / HERBERT BLOMSTEDT

⊙ Decca 460 988-2DF2 + ➡

Herbert Blomstedt clearly loves Nielsen's music and with his San Francisco orchestra on top form he gives thrilling performances of Symphonies Nos 4-6. The opening of *The Inextinguishable* is particularly fine as Blomstedt isn't frightened of letting things rip. He encourages an icily cool sound from the orchestra which is perfect for this music, and the timpani duel at the end is splendidly handled.

If you like this, try: Nielsen's Symphony No 5 • Nielsen's Helios Overture • Sibelius's Symphony No 5 • Shostakovich's Symphony No 4 • Prokoviev's Symphony No 3

CARMINA BURANA
(1937)
The most popular choral work of the 20th century?

The words for what the composer descibed as a "scenic cantata" are taken from an anthology of 13th-century student poems found in the monastery of Benediktbeuren in Bavaria. They're in Latin and German – bawdy celebrations of drinking, sex and other delights – and the music Orff gave them matches their spirit… raw, rhythmic, energetic, a fusion of traditional, jazz and contemporary techniques, some sounding almost "minimalist", long before that concept was even dreamed up. "O Fortuna", the powerful opening chorus, is now forever linked to a well-known brand of after-shave thanks to a long-running TV commercial in the 1980s! It's one of the most performed off all choral works of the 20th century.

80

Though known for a single work, Orff (1895-1982) was an influential educator and more versatile than his reputation suggests.

Coming from a musical family, the young Orff had his first works published when he was 16 and in just six months of 1911 wrote more than 50 songs; he flirted with the ideas of Schoenberg and the works of Richard Strauss but by the early 1920s had yet to find his own voice. He met Dorothee Günther in 1924 and together they founded the Günther Schule in Munich with the belief that everyone has an innate musical understanding and that movement and music cannot be separated. From his teaching, his interest in primitive rhythms and simple, monodic melodies led him to present imaginative stagings of Monteverdi, Schütz and Bach and his masterpiece, *Carmina Burana*.

Though the work's character appealed to Nazi sensibilities, Orff's radicalism and ideal of artistic communality did not and his methods were banned from German schools. His involvement with the regime is still open to question: like Richard Strauss, he wrote music for the 1936 Olympics (a Nazi showcase) and for *A Midsummer Night's Dream* to replace that of the outlawed Mendelssohn. Orff was much sniffed at by the critics while Stravinsky called his music, with its lack of thematic development and polyphony, "Neo-Neanderthall". After the War, Orff married the anti-Nazi author Luise Rinser and his teaching methods were given fresh impetus. He continued composing, though only *Catulli Carmina* (1943) emulates the style of *Carmina Burana*. He survived long enough to write music for the 1972 Munich Olympics.

The recording

**GUNDULA JANOWITZ
GERHARD STOLZE
DIETRICH FISCHER-DIESKAU
CHORUS & ORCHESTRA OF THE
DEUTSCHE OPERA, BERLIN /
EUGEN JOCHUM**

⊙ DG 447 437-2GOR + ⮑

Now superbly remastered, one can hear why this performance has consistently been a recommendation. Jochum pays great attention to detail – particularly with regard to tempo and articulation – yet the performance as a whole has a tremendous cogent sweep and the choruses have terrific power.

If you like this, try: Orff's Catulli Carmina • Prokofiev's Alexander Nevsky • Walton's Belshazzar's Feast • Steve Reich's Desert Music • John Adams's Harmonium

Until 1980, Arvo Pärt's music was unknown in the West. Though sometimes pigeon-holed as a minimalist composer with the likes of Adams, Glass and Reich, the hypnotic repetitions in his music offer something more profoundly spiritual.

Pärt is the first Estonian composer to achieve international recognition. Although his country was an independent Baltic state at the time of his birth in 1935, it was occupied by the Soviet Union from 1940 until 1991. After national service, when he was a side-drummer in an army band, from 1958 Pärt studied composition at the Conservatory in Estonia's capital, Tallinn. Pärt then worked as a recording engineer for the state radio station (1958-67), a role which led to an opportunity to write film scores. To date, he has composed over 50.

The first phase of his career brought him into conflict with the Soviet authorities for the music he wrote using serial and collage techniques. He finally abandoned these methods and underwent a voluntary period of compositional silence, during which he meditated, studied religion and the choral works of the 14th-16th centuries. His music emerged quite differently: "I have discovered it is enough when a single note is beautifully played," he has said. "This one note, or a moment of silence comforts me. I work with very few elements – with one voice, with two voices. I build with primitive materials – with the triad, with one specific tonality. The three notes of a triad are like bells. And that is why I call it tintinnabulation." The result is music of undramatic, uneventful, monk-like simplicity once described as "the most beautiful sound next to silence".

After constant struggles with the Soviet authorities, Pärt emigrated with his wife and two sons to Vienna where he took Austrian citizenship, and thence to Berlin where he now lives.

CANTUS IN MEMORIAM BENJAMIN BRITTEN (1980)
A powerful early example of Pärt's tintinnabuli style

Pärt's empathy with the "unusual purity of [Britten's] music" inspired this tribute for string orchestra and a single bell. Typically lasting just over six minutes, it is an early example of Pärt's tintinnabuli style, its material derived from a descending scale played simultaneously at three different speeds. Pärt was particularly affected by news of Britten's death, for here he felt was a kindred spirit and his passing had robbed him of the long-held ambition to meet him personally. Other effective works by Pärt are *De Profundis* (1980) for male choir, organ and percussion, notable for the relentless thumping of the bass drum which has been likened to "a primevel heartbeat" (the words are a setting of Psalm 130), *Summa* (1977), a setting of the Creed, and *The Beatitudes* (1990, rev 1991).

81

The recording

ESTONIAN NATIONAL SYMPHONY ORCHESTRA / PAAVO JÄRVI
⊙ Virgin Classics 545501-2 + ⮥

Pärt's mature music responds most readily to luminous textures, carefully timed silences and mastery of line, and only rarely to the more subjective impulses of dramatic conducting. Which isn't to say that there aren't significant differences between recordings, and Järvi conducts a superb programme here, opting for warmer textures than some rivals, which usefully underlines Part's quietly cascading harmonies.

If you like this, try: Pärt's Summa • Pärt's Spiegel im Spiegel • Pärt's De Profundis • Tavener's Song for Athene • Britten's Four Sea Interludes • Glass's Satyagraha

POULENC

ORGAN CONCERTO
(1938)
One of very few successful fusions of organ and orchestra

Arguably the most successful of all Poulenc's works, the Organ Concerto is unlike any other you've heard. With its thunderous opening chords and general air of gloom you think you're in for a hard time – and then suddenly you're in the variety theatre listening to music that couldn't be more carefree and exuberant. The concerto, in one continuous movement, changes from the sacred to the secular and back again reflecting Poulenc's own inner nature. Fun or tragic, he never stays in the same mood for long. Poulenc has worn well for all his derivative, lightweight reputation. Audiences like listening to it and musicians love playing it which, in the end, are the only reasons for music's survival. Why write music that no one wants to hear and no one enjoys playing?

82

One of his friends described Poulenc (1899-1963) as "half monk, half guttersnipe", which goes halfway to describing his music.

Poulenc's father was a wealthy pharmaceutist. His mother gave Francis his first piano lessons. In 1916, he continued these with one of the most respected pianists of the day, the Spanish Ricardo Viñes. Years later, Poulenc admitted "I owe him everything…it's really to Viñes that I owe my first flights in music and everything I know about the piano." Viñes introduced him to the father-figure of the French avant-garde, Eric Satie. Shortly afterwards, Poulenc had his first composition published, *Rhapsodie nègre* (1917). Overnight he was at the centre of the Parisian group of composers who came to be known as "Les Six", along with Auric, Durey, Honegger, Milhaud and Tailleferre.

After service in the French army (1918-21), he composed his popular *Trois mouvements perpétuels* while on the Vosges front – he decided to take his musical education a little more seriously, but not too seriously: one of the charms of Poulenc's music is that it is untainted by pre-conceived ideas. He embraced the flamboyant social life of 1920s Paris, producing a string of expertly crafted, witty, tuneful scores. Ballet commissions from Diaghilev, piano pieces of charm and elegance and, especially, songs, flowed from his pen. In this latter field, he found his ideal interpreter in the gifted baritone Pierre Bernac. In 1935, Poulenc's religious faith was revived and, while never abandoning his role as the worldly, chic jester, a religious vein recurs through the remainder of his music. His final works were the Oboe Sonata written in memory of Prokofiev and the Clarinet Sonata. He died suddenly in Paris in the same year that claimed Jean Cocteau and Paul Hindemith (1963).

The recording

**PHILIPPE LEFEBVRE
LILLE SYMPHONY ORCHESTRA /
JEAN-CLAUDE CASADESUS**

⊙ Naxos 8.554241 + ⊫

The recording technicians have skilfully succeeded in producing a string sonority that doesn't suffer beside the organ's awesome thunders. You can't help wondering whether Poulenc really had such a giant sound in mind, but it's undeniably thrilling; and the quieter moments are captured with commendable clarity and calm. This is an eminently recommendable disc.

DDD
8.554241

POULENC

Organ Concerto
Concert Champêtre
Suite française

Philippe Lefebvre
at the Great Organ
of Notre-Dame de Paris
Elisabeth Chojnacka
Harpsichord
Orchestre National de Lille
Jean-Claude Casadesus

If you like this, try: Poulenc's Les biches • Poulenc's Concert champêtre • Ibert's Divertissment • Walton's Façade • Martinů's Revue de cuisine

SERGEY PROKOFIEV

Born Sontzovka 1891 **Died** Moscow 1953

Prokofiev was the dominant force among domiciled Russian composers during the 1930s and '40s. He died on the same day as Stalin. Apart from the final years of his life, he managed more successfully than any other Russian composer living under the dictatorship to maintain his musical ideals.

Prokofiev was a brilliant student. By the age of 13 when he entered the St Petersburg Conservatoire he was already a good pianist and had produced an opera (aged nine), an overture and other works. He had the best teachers including Glière, Liadov and Rimsky-Korsakov. Anna Essipova (who had been married to one of the greatest piano teachers of the 19th century, Theodor Leschetizky) taught Prokofiev piano. Such a precocious, blazing talent inevitably rebelled against the stifling conservatism that confronted him.

Like Shostakovich and Britten, his style seemed to be pre-formed, completely original and one which remained constant for his entire creative life. Even before graduation, he caused a stir in musical circles with some of his compositions – the First Piano Concerto, with its violent keyboard gymnastics, unexpected harmonic, melodic twists and angular rhythms, caused a furore when it was first played. Before he was 20, Prokofiev was famous. But he was no wunderkind who burns out after initial brilliance.

In 1918 he left Russia and travelled through Siberia to Japan and America giving concerts of his own music and in 1920 arrived in Paris. Here, he met another ex-patriot, Sergei Diaghilev, who commissioned three ballets from him. Further commissions came from his publisher Koussevitzky and in 1921 he visited America again for the premiere of his opera *The Love for Three Oranges*.

After returning to Russia in 1927, where he was greeted as a celebrity, he flitted between his mother country, Paris

and other European cities before deciding in 1932 to settle in Russia for good. Why did he not live and work abroad in peace like Stravinsky and Rachmaninov? Perhaps he thought he was famous enough to be treated differently by the authorities. In this he was sadly mistaken and, after an initial period of co-habitation, the authorities and Prokofiev were at loggerheads. Nevertheless, some of his finest music was written in the 1930s and during the war years, despite increasing ill-health and the break up in 1941 of his marriage. Some pieces like "The Montagues and Capulets" from *Romeo and Juliet* have achieved the status of classical pops while others, like the Third Piano Concerto, *Lieutenant Kije* suite and the *Classical* symphony are central repertoire works.

When, in 1948, the Central Committee of the Communist Party denounced Prokofiev, Shostakovich and others for "formalism" – music that had no immediate function and did not extol the virtues of the wonderful Stalinist regime – a humiliating public apology appeared: "We are tremendously grateful to the Central Committee of the All-Union Communist Party and personally to you, dear Comrade Stalin, for the severe but profoundly just criticism of the present state of Soviet music...We shall bend every effort to apply our knowledge and our artistic mastery to produce vivid realistic music reflecting the life and struggles of the Soviet people." Thereafter, in the few years left to him, Prokofiev churned out inconsequential scores, the equivalent of the paintings of tractors and chemical works that Soviet artists were turning out.

83

PIANO CONCERTO NO 3
(1921)

A work that reveals so many of Prokofiev's myriad gifts

The most frequently played of Prokofiev's concertos and among the most popular 20th-century works in that form. The solo part is particularly brilliant with the strongly percussive element so characteristic of Prokofiev's piano music much in evident, but not without a stream of lyrical themes. It has three movements, the second consisting of a theme and five variations. The composer himself was the soloist for the premiere in Chicago (December 1921) and later made a revealing recording of the work though the sound is somewhat dim. There are four other piano concertos, No 1 (which caused such a stir when he was a student) is well worth trying next; No 4, for the left hand alone, was commissioned by the one-armed pianist Paul Wittgenstein, who never played it (too difficult!).

84

The recording

**VLADIMIR ASHKENAZY
LONDON SYMPHONY ORCHESTRA
/ ANDRÉ PREVIN**

⊙ Decca 452 588-2DF2 + ⇨

While it's true that the Prokofiev piano concertos are an uneven body of work, there's enough imaginative fire and pianistic brilliance to hold the attention even in the weakest of them; the best, by common consent Nos 1, 3 and 4, have stood the test of time very well. As indeed have these Decca recordings.

Ashkenazy has rarely played better. Other pianists have matched his brilliance and energy, but very few have kept up such a sure balance of fire and poetry. So many facets of Prokofiev's genius are here, and Ashkenazy shows how they all take their place as part of a kind of fantastic story.

LILLIAN BIRNBAUM/DG

If you like this, try: Shostakovich's Piano Concerto No 1 • Prokofiev's Violin Concerto No 2 • Prokofiev's Piano Sonatas Nos 7-9 • Rodion Shchedrin's Carmen Ballet

PROKOFIEV ESSENTIALS

Romeo and Juliet, ballet (1935)

The first production of this ballet based on Shakespeare's *Romeo and Juliet* was not a success. The Soviet critics found the music "hard, cold and incongruous" – and they disapproved of the happy ending Prokofiev had provided (he later restored the tragic one). It was not until he transformed the ballet score into three suites for the concert hall that the music caught on.

Violin Concerto No 2 in G minor (1935)

One of the 20th-century's greatest violin concertos, this has a slow movement that ranks as one of Prokofiev's loveliest creations. Its string of memorable themes (with, of course, Prokofiev's typically incisive, exciting rhythms) are unmistakably Russian, written in a warmer vein than even the Third Piano Concerto.

Peter and the Wolf (1936)

Prokofiev wrote this evergreen entertainment to teach children the sounds of the different instruments of the orchestra (the bird is a flute, the duck an oboe, the cat a clarinet and so on). A narrator speaks the text pausing to allow the music to give a tonal interpretation of what has just been described. The story was Prokofiev's own, though his music is far more imaginative than his prose which has been recorded by everyone from Sir Ralph Richardson and Dame Edna Everage to Sean Connery and Sting.

Classical Symphony (1917)

One of Prokofiev's most popular works, a delightful pastiche of the classical symphonies of Mozart and Haydn but with Prokofiev's own piquant harmonies, quirky, hummable themes and masterly economy of writing. An enjoyable introduction to neo-classicism.

SYMPHONY NO 5
(1944)

A symphony that manages to look both backwards and forwards

Like Prokofiev's sonatas for solo piano, the symphonies are not best heard one after the other: they are not all immediately accessible and to experience one after another can prove, let's say, "emotionally draining". The Fifth Symphony is probably the best loved of the seven he wrote. Composed within a single month in the summer of 1944, it is a hymn of praise to the spirit of man, a spirit that cannot be broken by war or oppression. After opening with a majestic slow movement and nervous, *scherzo*-like second, Prokofiev follows them with an *Adagio* of heart-rending intensity. It is among the finest things Prokofiev ever wrote. The last movement looks forward to the future with optimism.

85

The recording

BERLIN PHILHARMONIC ORCHESTRA / HERBERT VON KARAJAN

⊙ DG 463 613-2GOR + ⊟➔

Karajan proves to be a wonderful Prokofiev conductor, even if he draws a slightly denser sound from the orchestra than we're used to nowadays. His control of the long, sweeping melodies is superb and he clearly responds to the work's undercurrent of bitterness. The sound, on this 1968 recording, is opulent, spacious and full-bodied.

If you like this, try: Prokofiev's Symphony No 7 • Prokofiev's Cinderella • Borodin's Symphony No 2 • Mahler's Symphony No 7 • Sibelius's Symphony No 1

GIACOMO PUCCINI

Born Lucca 1858 **Died** Brussels 1924

Whatever the atmosphere he wanted to create, Puccini's sound world is unique and unmistakeable with its opulent yet clear-cut orchestration and a miraculous fund of melodies with their bittersweet, tender lyricism. His masterly writing for the voice guarantees the survival of his music for many years to come.

The fifth of seven children, Puccini was christened Giacomo Antonio Domenico Michele Secondo Maria, the fifth (and, as it turned out, the last) generation of a dynasty of Italian musicians. He studied piano and organ locally but it was not until a visit to Pisa in 1876 to see a production of *Aida* that he decided on a career as a musician. Studying at the Milan Conservatory, in 1883 he was encouraged by his teacher Amilcare Ponchielli, the composer of the opera *La Gioconda*, to enter a competition for a one-act opera. The result was *Le villi*. Though the work was not even mentioned when the prizes were announced, Puccini was heard singing extracts from it at a party. This led to a production of the work at the Theatro dal Verme in May 1884 which in turn led to the Italian publishing house of Ricordi snapping up the rights and commissioning Puccini to write another. He remained with the firm for the rest of his career.

Five years passed before he completed his next opera, *Edgar*. It was a failure, one of only two he experienced. During this time he began an affair with Elvira Gemignani. The couple would eventually marry only after Elvira's husband's death in 1904. Puccini's next subject for an opera was *Manon Lescaut* (1892). Overnight it made his name internationally famous.

Following this with *La bohème*, Puccini confirmed his promise as Verdi's heir-apparent. Within a short time *La bohème* had been produced all over the world.

With fame came wealth and in 1900 he built a fabulous villa in the simple village of Torre del Lago by the lake of Massaciuccoli, near Florence, and began work on his next project, based on Victorien Sardou's 1887 play *La Tosca*. Now one of the best-loved of operas with some of the most famous of all arias, *Tosca* divided the critics. Four years after *Tosca* came the third of this remarkable trilogy, *Madama Butterfly* (1904).

The Girl of the Golden West furnished Puccini with his next venture in the unlikely operatic setting of the 1849 Californian gold rush. It has never caught on in the same way as the previous three. His next work, *La Rondine*, was Puccini's second professional failure (it's an uneasy mix of opera and operetta). Challenging himself once more, Puccini then conceived the idea of an evening of three one-act operas: *Il Trittico* is made up of *Il Tabarro*, *Suor Angelica* and *Gianni Schicchi* – the latter by far the best of the three. Puccini's final opera presented even greater self-imposed challenges. Always abreast of the latest musical developments, Puccini incorporated into *Turandot* contemporary music techniques not normally associated with him. It was one of the last operas to have been written that has entered the standard repertoire and remained loved by the public at large. The composer himself never finished the score (the last two scenes were completed by Franco Alfano). Puccini died aged 65 from a heart attack while undergoing treatment for cancer of the larynx.

Maria Callas *Soprano*
The singer who brought
theatre into the opera house and
redefined operatic singing in the
1950s. Heard at her greatest in
Puccini's *Tosca* – see page 88

PHOTO • EMI ARCHIVES

PUCCINI ESSENTIALS

TOSCA
(1900)
An opera with three magnificent roles for three great actors

Puccini's third major success is the counterpart of *La bohème*, for while the music is no less ardent and lyrical, the love interest is sombre and tragic. Cavardarossi, the painter, is one of the great tenor roles, Tosca one of the most rewarding soprano roles, while Scarpia, the chief of police and one of opera's most believable villains, provides great acting opportunities for the baritone. Three particular arias stand out: "Recondita armonia" from Act 1 where Cavardarossi sings to the miniature he holds of Tosca; "Vissi d'Arte", Tosca's Act 2 outpouring when confronted with the possibility of surrendering herself to Scarpia; and "E lucevan le stelle", Cavaradossi's farewell, recalling his meetings with Tosca on starlit nights.

88

The recording

MARIA CALLAS; GIUSEPPE DI STEFANO; TITO GOBBI; CHORUS AND ORCHESTRA OF LA SCALA MILAN / VICTOR DE SABATA

⊙ EMI 562890-2 or 585644-2+ ➡
or Naxos 8 110256/7

One of the indisputable classics of the gramophone. Recorded in Milan in 1953 it finds the three principals on magnificent form. Callas simply is Tosca, and the range of colour she

brings to her singing is worthy of a great stage actress. Tito Gobbi is a fabulous

Scarpia – totally loathsome – and di Stefano an ardent Cavaradossi. De Sabata conducts magnificently.

If you like this, try: Puccini's Turandot • Puccini's Madama Butterfly • Bizet's Carmen • Offenbach's Tales of Hoffmann • Leoncavallo's Pagliacci

Madama Butterfly (1904)

Puccini came to London in 1900 and saw a production of David Belasco's play of the same title. Although he didn't understand a word, he was so deeply moved by what he saw that, according to the colourful and unreliable memoirs of Belasco, Puccini embraced the author and begged him for the rights with tears in his eyes. Belasco agreed at once and Puccini commenced work in the autumn of 1901. He himself felt that the work was "the most felt and most expressive opera that I have conceived" and it was his personal favourite of all his works. The story of the young geisha Cio-Cio San and her love for the US Navy's Lieutenant Pinkerton is a heart-breaker and contains such wonderful music as "Dolce notte" ("Sweet night"), the exquisite love duet at the end of Act 1; "Un bel dì vedremo" ("Someday he'll come" or "One Fine Day" as it's usually called), among the most popular soprano solos in all opera.

Turandot (1926)

There had been at least 10 other operas on the same subject written in the previous century, none of which had made any impression. Even Busoni's 1917 *Turandot* did not dissuade Puccini from using the same fairy tale in which Turandot, the bewitching daughter of the Chinese Emperor promises to marry any man of royal blood who can answer three riddles; he who fails to answer correctly is put to death. Those expecting the sound of *La bohème* and *Tosca* are in for a surprise, for here Puccini uses dissonance and polytonal vocal and orchestral passages. The result is, arguably, Puccini's most powerful dramatic work and one which combines the heroic, the comic and the lyrical in equal measure.

LA BOHÈME
(1896)
High passion, drama and heart-rending lyricism come together

You would not be the first person to become hooked on opera by being taken to see *La bohème* – it's a marvellous introduction to the whole experience, with some of music's best known arias and a touching tale of doomed love. There is high passion, drama and heart-rending lyricism: you have to be pretty hard of heart not to respond to Puccini's sumptuous score. Rodolfo's Act 1 "Che gelida manina" ("Your tiny hand is frozen") is one of the most popular of all tenor arias, while Mimì's answering "Sì, mi chiamano Mimì" ("Yes, they call me Mimì") is hardly less well loved. Then there's "Quando me 'n vo" ("When I am out walking") known as Musetta's Waltz Song and the melting quartet from Act 3 "Addio, dolce svegliare".

The recording

ANNA NETREBKO; ROLANDO VILLAZÓN; BAVARIAN RADIO SYMPHONY CHORUS AND ORCHESTRA / BERTRAND DE BILLY

⊙ DG 477 6600GH2 + ⇥

Vividly recorded, vigorously conducted and sung by a distinguished cast still in their relatively youthful prime, it presents the score with an appeal that will be readily felt by newcomers and with a freshness that will make those of riper years feel… well, feel young again.

KASSKARA/DG

If you like this, try: Puccini's Tosca • Puccini's Madama Butterfly • Puccini's Messa di Gloria • Verdi's Falstaff • Catalani's La Wally • Mascagni's Cavalleria Rusticana

PIANO CONCERTO NO 3
(1909)

One of the most demanding solo parts of any concerto

Despite the popularity of the Second Piano Concerto (of *Brief Encounter* fame), "Rach Three" (as it's known in the trade) is the more cleverly constructed piece of music: almost all the themes are inter-related with different versions of them cropping up in all three movements. It is also one of the most technically demanding solo parts of any concerto in the standard repertoire. With Rachmaninov's Russian melancholy, luxuriant orchestration and brilliant piano writing well to the fore, it is the epitome of the grand, late-romantic concerto. It was dedicated to Rachmaninov's friend, the great pianist Josef Hofmann who, nevertheless, never played it.

92

The recording

STEPHEN HOUGH
DALLAS SYMPHONY
ORCHESTRA / ANDREW LITTON
⊙ Hyperion CDA67501/2 + ↦
Stephen Hough recorded this set of the four Rachmaninov piano concertos and the *Paganini* Rhapsody live, and the electricity generated in those concert performances is palpable. In the Third Concerto, Hough manages wonderfully to convey the sense of struggle inherent in the music, and in the finale he's simply stupendous.

If you like this, try: Rachmaninov's Piano Concerto No 4 • Rachmaninov's Etudes-tableaux • Tchaikovsky's Piano Concerto No 1 • Prokofiev's Piano Concerto No 2

RACHMANINOV ESSENTIALS

Prelude in C sharp minor (1892) and 23 Preludes (1901-10)
In 1892, Rachmaninov wrote five short pieces for piano, his Op 3. The second of them is the C sharp minor Prelude which Rachmaninov nicknamed "It", because at every recital he gave he was forced to play "It". He grew to loathe "It". In a few pages it encapsulates much of Rachmaninov's mature style of music – the Slavic melancholy, Moscow church bells, plainsong chanting and a well-judged emotional climax. Rachmaninov wrote a further 23 Preludes: many display the same nostalgic yearning and Russian day-dreaming as the concertos.

Piano Concerto No 2 (1901)
After the disastrous premiere of his First Symphony, Rachmaninov entirely lost his creative urge and considered giving up composing altogether. He consulted a Dr Nikolai Dahl famous for his "magic cures", achieved by auto-suggestion. After daily visits from January to April 1900 for his course of "positive suggestion therapy" (hypnosis), Rachmaninov found that, miraculously, he could write again. The wonderful, soul-searching themes have endeared the concerto to millions – and many more when it was used to tissue-drenching effect in David Lean's 1945 film *Brief Encounter*. And it remains one of the most popular and most performed of all piano concertos.

Rhapsody on a theme of Paganini (1934)
The theme Rachmaninov takes is the famous A minor Caprice for solo violin by Paganini, the last of a set of 24 which revolutionised the instrument when they appeared in 1820. Rachmaninov's variations, which are played without a break, were written in 1934 while holidaying at his home on Lake Lucerne.

SYMPHONY NO 2
(1908)
One of Rachmaninov's greatest works without a piano!

One of Rachmaninov's most imposing and richly-rewarding works, the Second Symphony has had a far happier history than the disastrous First. It was completed a year before the Third Piano Concerto and its four movements follow the pattern, and to some extent the language, of a Tchaikovsky symphony. You can hear that many of the themes Rachmaninov uses are shared between different movements (for instance, there's a snatch of the first movement at the end of the third), a device which binds the whole work together. As in the *Paganini Rhapsody*, Rachmaninov introduces the tune of the *Dies Irae* (in the second movement). It's the *Adagio* (third movement) which enraptures the ear, though, with one of those searing, soaring melodies that only Rachmaninov could have written.

93

The recording

BUDAPEST FESTIVAL ORCHESTRA / IVÁN FISCHER

⊙ Channel Classics CCSSA21698 + ➡
Iván Fischer conducts the piece as Rachmaninov might have played it: with a free and malleable sense of spontaneity. It's the romantic more than the epic that Fischer emphasises.

Channel Classics has complemented his reading with a lovely, open and natural production. The blend is all Fischer's, though. Fischer's musical storytelling is exceptional. What do those sombre brass shadings tells us at the close of the *scherzo*? Rarely have they ever sounded quite so unsettling. Nor has the opening of the slow movement sounded more like Rachmaninov abruptly changing the subject. Fresh and engaging, then and well worth your attention – guaranteed to clear your head of preconceptions.

BUDAPEST FESTIVAL ORCHESTRA

If you like this, try: Rachmaninov's Isle of the Dead • Tchaikovsky's Symphony No 5 • Sibelius's Symphony No 4 • Elgar's Symphony No 1 • Prokofiev's Symphony No 5

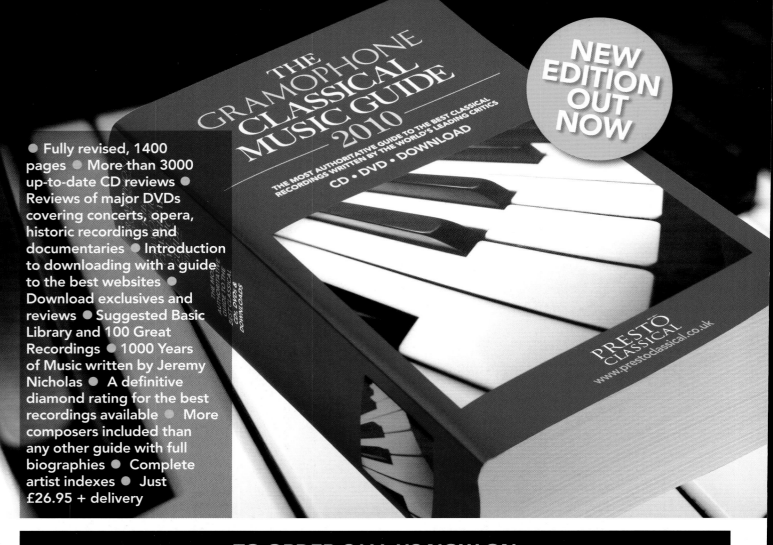

MAURICE RAVEL

Born Basses-Pyrénées 1875 **Died** Paris 1937

Ravel's greatest significance was in establishing, with Debussy, a distinct French school of music, ridding it of Wagnerian influence. One of the greatest orchestrators in musical history, he put it to use in music ranging from delicate impressionistic pictures to fantasies portraying children and animals.

Ravel's family moved to Paris when Maurice was three months old. His musical talent was encouraged, lessons began in 1882 when he was seven and he entered the Paris Conservatoire in 1889. Fauré was among his teachers and he remained a student for a further 16 years, an unusually long time. One reason for this was his strenuous attempts to win the coveted Prix de Rome. He was placed second in 1901, tried and failed in 1902 and 1903 and then was eliminated, humiliatingly, in 1905 before the final stage of the competition. The jury's decision became a *cause célèbre*, leading to the resignation of the Director of the Conservatoire, Théodore Dubois (Fauré took his place).

But by this time, Ravel was already a respected composer whose graceful *Pavane pour une Infante défunte*, piano piece *Jeux d'eau*, string quartet and *Shéhérazade* had been well received. When the scandal had died down, Ravel was famous. Over the next decade or so, he wrote some of his finest work, including *Rapsodie Espagnole*, *Gaspard de la Nuit*, and *Daphnis et Chloé*.

The First World War had a decisive and ultimately fatal effect on Ravel. His health up to that time had been good. However, the war broke him physically and emotionally. After being released from his duties as an ambulance driver because of dysentery, he was compelled to recuperate in hospital. His mother's death followed closely afterwards, deeply affecting him, and he began to suffer from insomnia and what he called "nervous debility". Thereafter, despite producing a number of masterpieces, inspiration came less frequently.

Ravel never married. Soon after the war he moved to a small villa called Belvédère about 30 miles to the south-west of Paris in Montfort-l'Amaury, living in semi-seclusion. All his affection was lavished on his beautiful home which, according to his biographer Madeleine Goss, "became his mother, wife and children…the only real expression of his entire life." There he lived with his housekeeper, a collection of mechanical and clockwork toys, and a family of Siamese cats (a passion he shared with Debussy). He accepted few pupils but gave friendly advice to many (including Vaughan Williams for three months); he never taught in any conservatory.

After Debussy's death in 1918 he was hailed as France's greatest living composer, honours were heaped upon him, though, perhaps in retaliation for the Prix de Rome debacle, he vehemently turned down the Légion d'honneur in 1920. In the autumn of 1932 he had a road accident in a Paris taxi from which he never fully recovered. The following year he began to notice difficulties in muscular coordination and he described his physical state as "living in a fog". Gradually, his memory went. Stravinsky, who described Ravel as "the perfect Swiss clockmaker", said: "Gogol died screaming, Diaghilev died laughing but Ravel died gradually – and that is the worst of all." An operation for a suspected brain tumour was decided upon. No tumour was found. Nine days later, having briefly regained consciousness, Ravel passed away.

INTRODUCTION AND ALLEGRO (1905)

To hear what is possible with this unusual combination is a revelation

Debussy once said of Ravel that he possessed "the finest ear that ever existed". Quite a compliment from such a fastidious critic, but listening to a work like this you can see why he said it. The *Introduction and Allegro* was written for the Parisian harpist Micheline Kahn and is scored for flute, clarinet, harp and string quartet. To hear what is possible with this small and unusual combination is a revelation – and all in the space of barely 11 minutes. After the slow introduction (one of the most atmospheric passages in chamber music) comes the *Allegro* and an extended harp solo, utilising the new chromatic harp, introduced in 1897.

If you like this, try: Ravel's String Quartet • Debussy's String Quartet • Saint-Saëns's piano trios • Messiaen's Quartet for the End of Time

96

The recording

**OSIAN ELLIS;
MELOS ENSEMBLE**
⊙ Decca 421 154-2DM + ⊕
The recording is a fine one for which no allowances have to be made even by ears accustomed to good digital sound; as for the work itself, this has an ethereal beauty that's nothing short of magical and Osian Ellis and his colleagues give it the most skilful and loving performance. A wonderful disc and a must-buy.

GASPARD DE LA NUIT
(1908)

Gaspard is among the greatest works ever written for the piano

Gaspard de la nuit is a collection of prose ballads by Aloysius Bertrand published in 1842, a year after his death at the age of 34. Their haunting Gothic imagery inspired Baudelaire, Mallarmé, Rimbaud – and Ravel. Choosing three of the ballads from the collection – "Ondine" (a water-spirit), "Le Gibet" (a musical portrait of the gallows) and "Scarbo" (a mischievous nocturnal imp) – Ravel sought to write a piano work of "transcendental virtuosity", as he described it. In this he succeeded (as any pianist will tell you!). *Gaspard* is not only Ravel's finest work for the piano but also among the greatest ever written for the instrument.

If you like this, try: Beethoven's "Moonlight" Sonata • Liszt's Sonata • Chopin's Preludes, Op 28 • Scriabin's Preludes • Messiaen's Preludes

The recording

ANGELA HEWITT
⊙ Hyperion CDA67341/2
Hewitt's *Gaspard* is a marvel of evocation through precision. Gone are old-fashioned vagueness and approximation: her "Le gibet" is surely among the most exquisitely controlled on record and her opening to "Scarbo" is alive with menace because all four of Ravel's directions are so precisely observed.

RAVEL ESSENTIALS

La valse (1919)
The score includes a written description of the progress of the music: "Whirling clouds give glimpses, through tiny chinks, of couples dancing. The clouds scatter, little by little. One sees an immense hall peopled with a twirling crowd. The scene is gradually illuminated. The light of the chandeliers bursts forth, fortissimo. An Imperial court, in or about, 1855." Or you could see it as an elegant Viennese waltz by Johann Strauss which gradually turns into a nightmare as the couples dance themselves to destruction.

Tzigane (1924)
Tzigane follows the pattern of a traditional Hungarian rhapsody: a long, slow introduction – a very difficult solo cadenza for the violin, played on the G-string (shades of Paganini) – leading to a fiery gypsy melody which, with other tunes and dances, culminates in a whirlwind finale. Ravel originally scored the work for violin and luthéal, a short-lived musical invention which was an organ-like attachment to the piano, but subsequently orchestrated the accompaniment.

Piano Concerto in G (1931)
Ravel explained he "conceived the concerto in the strict sense, written in the spirit of Mozart and Saint-Saëns". It took him two years to write but this brilliant masterpiece flashes by – its first movement gay and witty, the second as tender as a Mozart or Bach slow movement, the last with its emphasis on syncopated rhythm. Ravel obviously knew Gershwin's concerto - the whole work is heavily jazz influenced.

DAPHNIS ET CHLOE
(1912)

An extraordinary work – more like a vast symphony than a ballet

One of the 20th-century's landmark scores, this ballet was commissioned by Diaghilev for his Ballet Russe in 1909 with a story based on the mythical legend of Daphnis and Chloë. It took Ravel two years to complete this extraordinary work which is more like a vast symphony than a ballet. Strange to say, Diaghilev did not like the result and the premiere, danced by Nijnsky, was not a success. Nowadays you're more likely to hear this atmospheric, impressionistic music in the form of the two suites Ravel prepared from the full score. The second of these is the more popular and contains one of the great musical depictions of a sunrise with "Daybreak".

97

The recording

BERLIN PHILHARMONIC / PIERRE BOULEZ

⊙ DG 447 057-2GH + ⮕
Here Boulez has the Berlin Philharmonic Orchestra on top form to sustain and shape melody within some of his strikingly slow tempos (such as the opening, and Part 3's famous "Daybreak"), and who remain "composed" in his daringly fast ones (the "Dance of the young girls around Daphnis" and the "Danse guerrière" – one of the most exciting on disc).

If you like this, try: Ravel's Shéhérazade • Debussy's La mer • Stravinsky's The Rite of Spring • Tchaikovsky's Swan Lake • Schoenberg's Gurrelieder

Antonio Pappano *Conductor*
As well as his Respighi, Pappano, in his element in the opera house, conducts a superb *Tristan und Isolde* (page 144) and a magnificent Verdi Requiem (page 140)

PHOTO • CLIVE ARROWSMITH

RESPIGHI

The symphonic field was one which Italian composers had neglected for years in favour of opera. Respighi was an orchestrator of genius.

Respighi (1879-1936) began by studying the violin and viola in Bologna. In 1900 he went to Russia where he played first viola in the Imperial Opera orchestra in St Petersburg. Here he took lessons from Rimsky-Korsakov, who proved to be a decisive influence on his compositional style, though one can also hear the influence of Debussy and Richard Strauss. In 1902 he spent some time in Berlin studying with Max Bruch and continued his career as a violin soloist and as viola player with the Mugellini Quartet of Bologna. He was made a professor of composition at the Santa Cecilia Academy in Rome in 1913 and appointed its director ten years later.

His works may lack the ultimate in individuality but it was he and Busoni who revived Italy's instrumental tradition. All his scores are notable for their imaginative, luscious harmonies and "sound colour" with a love of splashy, flamboyant effects. A good place to start is with his *Ancient airs and dances* (1917-33). Here he applies his skill to three suites of orchestral transcriptions of short pieces originally written for the lute.

Respighi toured the United States in 1926 as composer and pianist, returning in 1928 for a performance of his opera *The Sunken Bell* at the Met and again in 1932 for his "mystery" *Mary of Egypt* at Carnegie Hall. The same year, Respighi and nine other Italian composers signed a manifesto condemning composers of cerebral music. "We are against this art which cannot have and does not have any human content," they protested, "and desires to be merely a mechanical demonstration and a cerebral puzzle."

After a long illness, Respighi died of a heart attack.

ROMAN TRILOGY
(1914-16, 1924 & 1928)
Italy's first great purely orchestral score?

Respighi's major works are three evocative musical portraits of the Eternal City, each one consisting of four separate symphonic poems. *Fontane di Roma* (1914-16: "The Fountains of Rome") is generally considered to be the best with each Roman fountain "contemplated at the hour in which their character is most in harmony with the surrounding landscape" (Respighi). *Pini di Roma* (1924), the second in the series, celebrates "the century-old trees which dominate so characteristically the Roman landscape…testimony for the principal events in Roman life". The four movements of *Feste romane* (premiered by Toscanini in 1928) depict four very different kinds of festivals, all painted in Respighi's lush and imaginative orchestration.

99

The recording

SANTA CECILIA ACADEMY ORCHESTRA, ROME / ANTONIO PAPPANO

⊙ EMI 394429-2 + ↦

Conducting the orchestra of the Roman institution that Respighi used to direct, Antonio Pappano serves up these firm favourites in great sound and with some exuberant playing. This is music that teeters on the vulgar, and the art is to keep it a few degrees from sounding as if it were written for Hollywood. Pappano does a great job, and the EMI sound is most impressive.

If you like this, try: Respighi's Brazilian Impressions • Respighi's Church Windows • Villa-Lobos's Bachianas Brasileiras • Ravel's Daphnis et Chloé • Rozsa's Ben Hur

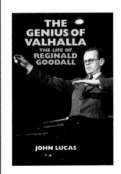

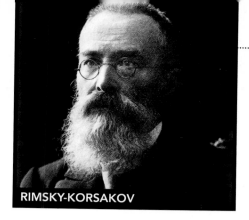

RIMSKY-KORSAKOV

Despite the meagre amount of his music heard regularly today, Rimsky-Korsakov's place in Russian music cannot be overstated.

Music was part of the fabric of Rimsky's wealthy, aristocratic, landed family and he was discovered to have a natural talent for the piano at an early age. But his one ambition was to join the navy like his elder brother, entering the Naval School in St Petersburg in 1856. Meanwhile he took piano lessons and began to form ideas for composition. He was introduced to Balakirev and, like many another, fell under his charismatic influence, cajoled into attempting a symphony. In time, Rimsky (1844-1908) would become the fifth and most important member of the group known as "The Mighty Handful" who were to shape the force of Russian nationalism in music.

On his return from the sea, Balakirev conducted a performance of Rimsky's Symphony No 1 which, as much as anything, finally determined him to make music his life. He was still considered as a gifted musical amateur by the circle in which he moved – and he was certainly musically under-educated. His astonishment can be imagined then, when, at the age of 27, he was offered the post of professor of composition at the St Petersburg Conservatory. He remained on the faculty from 1870 until his death. Instinct alone had got him thus far. Though still officially in the navy, Rimsky was made inspector of Russian military bands in 1873. From here on, Rimsky-Korsakov's history is one of increasing influence as a teacher and administrator, parallel with his development as one of Russia's most celebrated composers. Overwork brought him to the verge of a nervous breakdown in 1889 to be followed, after a relapse of two years, by a further creative outburst.

SCHEHERAZADE
(1888)
Oriental magic that has audiences entranced

Rimsky's most celebrated large-scale composition is based on episodes from Tales of the Arabian Nights. The Sultan, convinced of the faithlessness of women, is determined to kill each of his wives after the first night he spends with them. One of them, the Sultana Scheherazade, represented in the music by the solo violin, saves her life by diverting him with stories she relates over a period of one thousand and one nights. It was a subject that could have been dreamt up specially for Rimsky's special gifts – the exotic setting, the beguiling rhythms of the Orient and the fabulous stories are captured brilliantly in his multi-coloured orchestration. There are four separate movements in his symphonic suite at the end of which the Sultan speaks in a gentle, amorous tone – so everyone lives happily ever after.

101

The recording

KIROV ORCHESTRA / VALERY GERGIEV
Philips 470 840-2PH +

Recorded live, this is a red-blooded *Scheherazade* that emphasises the drama. Gergiev's orchestra, usually found playing opera, has a superbly rich, deep-red tone, and there are some very fine solosts among its ranks. Gergiev's recording soon makes us forget the stop-start nature of the work and sweeps everything along on a wave of story-telling as magnetic as that of the Sultana herself.

If you like this, try: Rimsky-Korsakov's Mlada • Balakirev's Tamara • Borodin's In the Steppes of Central Asia • Ravel's Shéhérazade • Ippolitov-Ivanov's Caucasian Sketches

RODRIGO

CONCIERTO DE ARANJUEZ
(1939)
For many, Spain in music

Having spent much of the previous decade in Paris, in 1939 Rodrigo and his wife moved to the princely town of Aranjuez, 48 kilometres south of Madrid, famous for its Palacio Real. Here he put the finishing touches to a guitar concerto that has firmly planted itself in the affection of music lovers like few other 20th-century works. It is a notoriously difficult combination to score the weak-toned guitar against a full orchestra, but Rodrigo pitched it perfectly. Has there ever been a more vivid musical picture of Spain than this? The sunshine and sangria are there but also nostalgia and heartache in the beautiful *Adagio*, memorably transformed by jazz trumpeter Miles Davis for his 1960 "Sketches of Spain" album.

102

Rodrigo's name is universally known as the composer of far and away the most popular guitar concerto ever written.

Rodrigo (1901-99) was born in Sagunto, Valencia, and became almost completely blind at the age of three after contracting diphtheria. He had an innate musical talent. At eight he began learning the violin and piano and at 19 was sent to study composition in Valencia for three years. Later he was taught by Paul Dukas, of *The Sorcerer's Apprentice* fame, in Paris. Here he met and was encouraged by his compatriot Manuel de Falla. In 1933 he married the Turkish pianist Victoria Kamhi and returned briefly to Spain but went back to Paris on a grant to study musicology with Maurice Emmanuel and André Pirro. He returned to his native country only after the end of the Civil War.

His attitude to the Franco regime is ambiguous. Friends assert he merely paid lip-service to the dictatorship; others say his views were those of Franco's government. At any rate, especially after the premiere of the *Concierto de Aranjuez*, he was a favoured son of the administration. In 1944 he was made music advisor to Spanish Radio and in 1947 was made professor of music history, holding the Manuel de Falla Chair of Music at the University of Madrid, a post created specially for him.

The *Concierto* led to many commissions from distinguished musicians including concertos for James Galway and Julian Lloyd Webber. The most successful of these was the *Fantasía para un gentilhomme* for the great guitarist Andrés Segovia written in 1954. Despite Rodrigo's tendency to repeat the successful formula of the *Concierto de Aranjuez*, it was he alone who kept the identity of Spanish classical music alive in the Franco era.

The recording

NORBERT KRAFT
NORTHERN CHAMBR ORCHESTRA /
NICHOLAS WARD

⊙ Naxos 8.550729 + ▶

Partnered by concertos by Castelnuovo-Tedesco and Villa-Lobos, this is a very fine performnace of Rodrigo's eternally popular concerto. Kraft plays it straight, not over-indulging in Rodrigo's great tunes, but allowing the music itself to weave the magic. The NCO are excellent partners and the recording handles the difficult balance between guitar and orchestra very well.

RODRIGO
Concierto de Aranjuez
Villa-Lobos: Guitar Concerto
Castelnuovo-Tedesco: Guitar Concerto No. 1

Norbert Kraft, Guitar
Northern Chamber Orchestra
Nicholas Ward, Director

If you like this, try: Rodrigo's Fantasía para un gentilhombre & Concierto en modo galante • Villa-Lobos's Guitar Concerto • Castelnuovo-Tedesco's Guitar Concerto

GIOACHINO ROSSINI

Born Pesaro 1792 **Died** Paris 1868

"Delight must be the basis and aim of this art," Rossini wrote. "Simple melody – clear rhythm!" Rossini's contribution to the development of opera was immense, indeed his works dominated the opera world for the first half of the 19th century. Where he led, Donizetti and Bellini followed.

Rossini's father was the town trumpeter for Pesaro who doubled as the municipal inspector of slaughterhouses; his mother was a small-time opera singer. Rossini's gifts showed themselves early so that when he reached his teens he could not only play the piano, the viola and the horn but was much in demand as a boy soprano.

By the time he left the Liceo Musicale in Bologna in 1810 he had composed a large amount of music including six string sonatas and his first opera *Demetrio e Polibio* (1806). This led to his first commission – *La cambiale di matrimonio*, a one-act opera which in turn prompted further commissions. From here Rossini's career snowballed rapidly. His first full-length opera *Tancredi* was an enormous success and less than three months later he had an even greater triumph with his comic opera *L'Italiana in Algeri* ("The Italian Girl in Algiers"). By 21 he was famous throughout Italy.

Venice had been the stage for his early work. Rossini then moved on to Naples and temporarily to Rome to write an opera for the Teatro Argentina. He decided to use Beaumarchais' play *Le Barbier de Séville*, despite the fact that there were at least four other musical versions of the play doing the rounds. The result was a comic masterpiece. Based in Naples, Rossini began an affair with the prima donna Isabella Colbran and continued his extraordinary progress with *La Cenerentola* (1817), *Mosè in Egitto* (1818), *La Gazza Ladra* ("The Thieving Magpie", 1817) and *Zelmira*

(1822). In fact, between 1808 and 1829 he produced no fewer than 40 operas. Now married to Colbran, Rossini moved to Vienna where he composed *Semiramide* (1823), his next big hit. Then on to London where he was fêted by public and royalty alike (George IV sang duets with him) and was hailed as the greatest living composer.

In 1824 he headed for Paris where he adapted his style to French tastes with *Le Comte Ory* (1828) following it with his grand opera masterpiece *William Tell*. That was in 1829. Rossini was by now immensely wealthy and at the height of his creative powers. Then he simply stopped composing. Except for his *Stabat mater* and *Petite Messe Solennelle* of 1863, he wrote nothing else of importance. Though it is known he suffered from depression for 20 years, no one has yet come up with a completely convincing explanation why he made this decision. In 1832 Rossini met Olympe Pélissier, a celebrated Parisian beauty, who became his mistress. They left Paris for Bologna in 1836 and, when Isabella Colbran died in 1845, the two were married.

They lived in Florence and in 1855 returned to Paris. Renowned for his hospitality, Rossini made his home the focal point for the great artists of the day.

Like many Italians, Rossini was superstitious and was terrified of Friday 13th. He died on Friday November 13, 1868. There were 6000 mourners in his funeral procession, four military bands and a chorus of 399. His estate was valued at about one million pounds.

103

THE BARBER OF SEVILLE
(1816)
"It will be played as long as opera exists" (Beethoven)

It has been described as "the best comic opera ever written" and that might well be right. Since its second performance in February 1816 (the first night was a fiasco) "The Barber" has kept its place in the popularity stakes. It's based on one of three popular plays by Beaumarchais concerning the lovable rogue Figaro, the barber of the title (see also Mozart's *The Marriage of Figaro*). The miracle is that Rossini wrote the entire score (600 pages of it) in just 13 days according to the composer (19 according to his biographer), an incredible feat even if he did self-plagiarise from earlier works. Singers relish the splendid opportunities, especially the mezzo or soprano appearing as Rosina. The Overture and many of the opera's individual arias are loved even by those who have never heard a complete opera. Act 1 alone includes "Ecco ridente", "Largo al factotum" and "Una voce poco fa".

The recording

THOMAS ALLEN; AGNES BALTSA; FRANCISCO ARAIZA; ACADEMY OF ST MARTIN IN THE FIELDS / SIR NEVILLE MARRINER

⊙ Philips 470 434-2DOC2 + ▷

A multi-national cast wth hardly a native Italian-speaker in sight, but it works terrifically well, with Thomas Allen proving what a magnificent vocal actor he is, and Agnes Baltsa sending up showers of vocal sparks with her vivacity and fizz. And Neville Marriner, a relative newcomer to opera, paces everything with a real dramatic feel. A truly infectious production.

If you like this, try: Rossini's L'Italiana in Algeri • Rossini's La Cenerentola • Mozart's The Marriage of Figaro • Mozart's Così fan tutte • Verdi's Falstaff

ROSSINI ESSENTIALS

La Cenerentola ("Cinderella", 1817)

Pronounced La Chay-nay-ren'tow-lah, this is Rossini's setting of the same story we know from pantomime. Like *The Barber*, it's full of quick-fire invention, patter songs, brilliant ensembles and thrilling coloratura solos. Act 2 has the famous Rondo aria "Non più mesta" with which Cinderella forgives her stepsisters and finishes the opera.

William Tell, overture (1829)

Though known as the most famous opera overture of all – indelibly associated by people of a certain age with *The Lone Ranger* – it is rather more than that, for it is actually a miniature symphonic poem, the nearest Rossini ever came to formally producing one independent of an opera. Berlioz described it as "a work of immense talent which resembles genius so closely as to be mistaken for it". It is in four sections: a picture of sunrise over the Swiss mountains leading to a storm and a lovely pastoral section. Trumpet calls herald the arrival of the Swiss army and the celebrated gallop which ends this masterpiece.

Stabat mater (1832)

Subdivided into ten sections, this work is written for four soloists, chorus and orchestra. When finally performed in the version by which we know it today, some thought it superior even to Haydn's *The Creation* and, when Donizetti conducted an early performance, the audience surrounded Rossini's apartment demanding his appearance to acknowledge the ovation. The exalted melodies and the immense skill with which the voices are handled make for an inspiring work. The second section includes "Cujus animam", a brilliant tenor solo.

OVERTURES
(1813-29)
Some of opera's most perfect comic miniatures

No record collection is complete without a disc of Rossini overtures, most of them far more familiar to audiences than the operas which they precede. The best of these are the Overtures to *L'Italiana in Algeri* ("The Italian Girl in Algiers", 1813) which introduces "the Rossini *crescendo*" – a short, fast passage repeated over and over, each time with fuller orchestration; *La Cenerentola* ("Cinderella", 1817); *La scala di seta* ("The Silken Ladder", 1812) and *Il Signor Bruschino* (1812 & 1813), the latter containing a passage where the violins are requested to play with the wood of their bows instead of the hair; *La gazza ladra* ("The Thieving Magpie",1817) – opening with an arresting roll on two snare drums before a grand, vigorous march; *Semiramide* (1823) – a masterpiece and one of the few in which Rossini uses material from the opera itself.

105

The recording

NATIONAL PHILHARMONIC ORCHESTRA / RICCARDO CHAILLY

⊙ Decca 443 8502DF2 + ⮥
All the favourites are here played by an orchestra that has recorded many Rossini operas and a conductor who knows his way around Rossini's stage works. Chailly brings out the variety, the poetry and above all the sense of anticipation in these incredibly

clever small-scale creations.

If you like this, try: Mozart's overtures • Weber's overtures • Rossini's The Barber of Seville • Rossini's Introduction, Theme and Variations for Clarinet and Orchestra

CAMILLE SAINT-SAËNS

Born Paris 1835 **Died** Algiers 1921

Saint-Saëns was one of the most remarkable prodigies – indeed, he had an altogether remarkable mind: organist, pianist, conductor, caricaturist, dabbler in science, mathematics and astronomy, traveller, archaeologist, writer of plays, philosophist, essayist on botany and ancient music.

Saint-Saëns began playing the piano at two-and-a-half, gave a performance in a Paris salon at 5, began to compose at 6, and made his official debut aged 10. As an encore he offered to play any one of Beethoven's 32 sonatas from memory. His First Symphony appeared in 1853. As a pianist and organist of exceptional ability he was much in demand and at the age of 22 he secured the most prestigious organ post in France at the Madeleine. Here he developed his legendary gifts for improvisation – Liszt called him the greatest organist in the world. Hans von Bülow rated Saint-Saëns "the greatest musical mind of our time."

As well as touring extensively as a pianist, both in solo concerts and in performances of his own piano concertos, he became a professor of piano at the Ecole Niedermeyer in 1861 and ten years later helped found the Société Nationale, dedicated to the performance of music by French composers. He composed at tremendous speed: his *Oratorio de Noël* was completed in 12 days; for a commission he had forgotten about he produced 21 pages of full score in two hours; the popular Second Piano Concerto took three weeks from start to finish.

By the late 1860s Saint-Saëns was numbered amongst the top few great living composers and awarded the Légion d'Honneur at only 33. His private life was not so fortunate. He was 40 when he married the 19-year-old Marie Truffot, sister of one of his pupils. The couple had two children but Saint-Saëns had little time for family life and in the first three years of his marriage completed his opera *Samson et Dalila*, his Piano Concerto No 4, the oratorio *Le Déluge*, a suite for orchestra, a symphonic poem, made a visit to Russia (where he became close friends with Tchaikovsky), composed numerous other short works, gave concerts and, in the spring of 1878, returned from Switzerland after writing a Requiem Mass.

The day he arrived home coincided with a terrible tragedy. His two-and-a-half year old son had fallen out of a fourth-floor window; barely six weeks later, his second son died suddenly. Three years after that, Saint-Saëns and his wife were on holiday. Without warning, he disappeared and, though they never divorced, he never saw his wife again. Marie Saint-Saëns died aged nearly 95 in January 1950.

In December 1888 Saint-Saëns's mother died, the only person to whom he was ever really close. After 1890, he wrote very little of consequence and began to indulge in his passion for foreign travel with visits to the USA, Colombo and Saigon and frequent trips to the Canary Islands and Algeria. As his music became less and less appreciated by the coming generation, he became proportionately more irritable but, though an arch-conservative, remained the Grand Old Man of French music. He was still giving recitals three months before his death (he went on a concert tour of Algiers and Greece at the age of 85). When he announced his retirement in August 1921, he had been before the public for 75 years.

SAINT-SAËNS ESSENTIALS

Introduction and Rondo Capriccioso (1863)

This is the earliest of Saint-Saëns's concert works for violin, composed when he was 28 and dedicated to the Spanish virtuoso Pablo de Sarasate. It is in two sections, as the title suggests: a questioning, plaintive Introduction followed by the Rondo, among the composer's most instantly recognisable tunes. Described as "one of the golden apples of Saint-Saëns's tonal garden", the work demands the ultimate in classical poise and control – "grace under fire" is needed to bring it off successfully.

Danse macabre (1874)

Saint-Saëns's most famous orchestral tone poem was originally written as a song for voice and piano in 1873 to a poem by Henri Cazalis. The opening lines are: "Zig-a-zig-a-zig – hark! Death beats a measure, / Drums on a tomb with heels hard and thin". When Saint-Saëns transformed the song the following year into a purely orchestral work, he depicted skeletons rising from their graves at the stroke of midnight for a wild, ghostly dance. This rises to a climax, the strains of the *Dies Irae* are heard, the oboe imitates the cock crowing at dawn and the skeletons disappear into the mist.

The Carnival of the Animals (1886)

It's ironic that the most popular work by Saint-Saëns should be the one he never intended for publication. The only section he allowed to appear in print during his lifetime was "The Swan". Each creature in his *Grande Fantaisie Zoologique* allows him to exhibit pure musical craftsmanship and to send up the music of Rossini, Mendelssohn, Berlioz, Offenbach and himself (*Danse macabre*) to enchanting effect.

ARTHUR UMBOH/DG

SYMPHONY NO 3, "ORGAN"
(1886)
A grand, grand symphony

This glorious work – the "Saint-Saëns Organ Symphony" as it's generally called – was popularised by its use in the 1995 film *Babe*. The famous bit – where the full organ comes thundering in – is actually the same tune (played in a major key) as the tune at the very opening of the symphony (played in a minor key). And that opening theme is itself derived from the Latin plainchant *Dies Irae*. It crops up throughout the symphony in various guises, even in the reposeful slow movement when the organ makes its first appearance. Saint-Saëns dedicated this, the last of his three mature symphonies, to the memory of his friend Franz Liszt. It remains, with the Poulenc Concerto for organ, timpani and strings, one of very few works for symphony orchestra and organ still regularly performed today.

107

The recording

**SIMON PRESTON
BERLIN PHILHARMONIC
ORCHESTRA / JAMES LEVINE**
⊙ DG 419 617-2GH + ➡

A thrilling recording of this popular work that for once gets the balance right – rarely are the organ and the orchestra recorded in the same place at the same time. James Levine conducts quite a fierce performance but he also knows when to linger and relish Saint-Saëns's fabulous melodies. The disc also

contains a terrific performance of Dukas's *Sorcerer's Apprentice*.

If you like this, try: Poulenc's Concerto for organ, timpani and strings • Widor's Toccata • Liszt's Les préludes • Bruckner's Te Deum • Janáček's Glagolitic Mass

PIANO CONCERTO NO 2
(1868)
A work that gives a glimpse of the multi-faceted Saint-Saëns

Saint-Saëns wrote five piano concertos, this one being the most popular, one in which Bach (in the first movement) meets Offenbach (in the last movement). Saint-Saëns produced it in just 17 days after the great Russian pianist/composer Anton Rubinstein, scheduled to conduct a concert in Paris, invited Saint-Saëns to appear as soloist. Although he managed to finish writing the concerto in time, Saint-Saëns had not mastered the extremely demanding solo part, and only the second movement (a *scherzo*) went off well. It's a work of ear-tickling delight from start to finish with its dramatic first movement, rumty-tumty Mendelssohn-like second and scorching tarantella finale.

108

The recording

STEPHEN HOUGH
CITY OF BIRMINGHAM SYMPHONY ORCHESTRA / SAKARI ORAMO
⊙ Hyperion CDA67331/2 + ⮕

As part of his complete cyle of all five piano concertos (voted as the public's favourite Record of the Year from the past 30 at the *Gramophone* Awards), Stephen Hough once again proves that he is unequalled in this repertoire. He has the technique, the wit, the imagination and the sense of the faintly absurd to carry it off. A totally wonderful set.

If you like this, try: Poulenc's piano concertos • Ravel's piano concertos • Tchaikovsky's Second Piano Concerto • Gershwin's Piano Concerto

SCHOENBERG

Schoenberg (1874-1951) may fairly be said to have been one of the most influential musicians in history with his advocacy of the 12-note technique.

Schoenberg's first two undoubted masterpieces, *Verklärte Nacht* (1899) and the mammoth *Gurrelieder* (1911) are two lusciously-scored, richly-romantic works in a post-Wagnerian style. From the early 1900s, he became increasingly adventurous. Frustrated by what he saw as the limitations of current musical language, he embraced what others had been hinting at: music that, for the first time, had no key – atonal music. It seemed to those listening as though they were being subjected to an assault of cacophonous, random, improvised notes.

Through his composition and teaching in Vienna, Schoenberg gradually won a reputation as a formidable musical thinker and attracted a group of devoted disciples who shared his experimental aims, a group that musical history now refers to as the Second Viennese School. After the First World War, discouraged by the lack of performances of his work, he formed the Society for Private Performances. Here his music and that of his followers could be heard in ideal conditions.

The rise of the Nazis ensured that he was dismissed from his post. Although born a Jew, he had converted to the Christian faith in 1898; moving to Paris in 1933, confronted with the German persecution of Jews, he reconverted to Judaism and left Europe for America, at the same time changing the spelling of his name from Schönberg to Schoenberg. He settled in Los Angeles where he taught at UCLA until 1944. In 1946 he had a near-fatal illness, after which his health declined rapidly.

VERKLÄRTE NACHT
(1899)
One of Schoenberg's last tonal works and an Expressionist gem

Now usually heard in the version the composer made for chamber orchestra in 1917, this string sextet is pre-atonal Schoenberg. It was inspired by the poem "Weib und di Welt" by the Symbolist poet Richard Dehmel, telling the story of a walk through a moonlit grove by a man and woman; the woman confesses she has been unfaithful and is to bear another man's child. The man forgives and forgets. Thus, through forgiveness, the world becomes transfigured. Not that you need to know the background to enjoy this deeply emotional, passionate and romantic score. In 1907, Schoenberg's wife Mathilde had an affair with a young painter, Richard Gerstl, who was living in their house. Friends persuaded her to return to her husband and two small children; Gerstl could not accept the situation and committed suicide aged 25.

109

The recording

BERLIN PHILHARMONIC ORCHESTRA / HERBERT VON KARAJAN

⊙ DG 457 721-2GOR + ⇒

This is the full-string option and Karajan, needless to say, uses a very large body of strings. But the textures he weaves and the colours he makes with his extraordinary orchestra are quite mesmerising. This may be a late-Romantic approach to the score but Karajan had an innate sympathy with

much modern music and he left a performance that has the power really to move the listener.

If you like this, try: Schoenberg's Song of the Wood Dove • Schoenberg's Chamber Symphonies • Berg's Violin Concerto • Wagner's Wesendonck-Lieder

Mark Padmore *tenor* &
Paul Lewis *piano*
Two wonderfully individual
musicans who make Schubert's
Winterreise a work of almost
unbearable intensity (page 114)

FRANZ SCHUBERT

Born Vienna 1797 **Died** Vienna 1828

Schubert was not the first of the Romantics but he was, as one writer put it, "the first lyric poet of music". The ideas came tumbling out like water from a spring. His gift for melody has, quite probably, never been equalled.

Schubert was the son of a modest schoolmaster. His mother was a cook. By the age of 10 Schubert could play the piano, organ, violin and viola. In 1808 he became a member of the Imperial Court chapel choir in Vienna which meant that his education, board and lodging at the Chapel School were paid for. Among his teachers was Salieri. "You can do everything," he announced to this timid, diffident little boy, "for you are a genius."

There has probably been no one in the history of music with such a prodigious facility as Schubert. Between 1813 and 1816 he composed five symphonies, four masses, several string quartets, stage music, an opera and some of his most famous lieder – *Gretchen am Spinnrade*, for example, written when he was just 17 and *Erlkönig* when he was 18 – songs of astonishing maturity and originality for which there was no precedence. In 1815 alone he composed no less than 140 songs (on October 15 he composed eight in one day!).

Three years later we find him supplementing his meagre income by teaching music to the daughters of Count Esterházy at his summer estate in Zelésk, Hungary. Unlike Haydn before him, there was no permanent post for him there; and unlike Beethoven, Schubert never found a rich (and permanent) patron. By 1820 he had composed over 500 works embracing every branch of composition. Yet only two of them had ever been heard in public – the Mass in F (in 1814) and one single solitary song (in 1819). The music commissioned for a play and

an opera were both critical flops and it wasn't until 1821 that his first work (a volume of songs) was published – and then only because his friends clubbed together to pay the costs.

Failure and lack of recognition began to bite hard. His incidental music to *Rosamunde* was accused of being "bizarre" and of his opera *Alfonso und Estrella*, Weber remarked dismissively, "First puppies and first operas should be drowned". Poverty and having to live on the charity of friends made him increasingly despondent. Added to this, he had to cope with the effects of venereal disease. "Each night when I go to sleep," wrote Schubert, "I hope never again to waken, and every morning reopens the wounds of yesterday." Yet in the midst of this, he wrote the *Unfinished* Symphony (1825) and in the last two years of his life some of the most divine music ever written – the String Quintet, the *Great* C major Symphony, the last three Piano Sonatas, the two Piano Trios, the Mass in E flat and the 14 songs that would be gathered together to from the cycle *Schwanengesang*.

On March 26, 1828 in the Musikverein of Vienna, there was given for the first time a programme entirely devoted to Schubert's music. Less than eight months later he died of typhoid, delirious, babbling of Beethoven. He was 31 and was buried as near to him as was practicable with the epitaph: "The art of music here entombed a rich possession, but yet fairer hopes." Schubert left no estate at all, absolutely nothing – except his manuscripts.

111

PIANO SONATA, D 960
in B flat (1828)
A must for all lovers of the Romantic piano repertoire

Schubert completed 21 sonatas for the piano. The last three of these, considered to be the best of the bunch, are known as the "posthumous sonatas" because, though written in 1828, they were not published until ten years after Schubert's death. The finest of these is the B flat Sonata, required playing for all pianists, required listening for all lovers of the piano. The first movement alone (observing repeats) lasts over 20 minutes; the slow movement has been described as among the greatest slow movements ever composed. It is profoundly personal music, written when Schubert was in the last year of his short life.

If you like this, try: Schubert's Piano Sonata, D959 • Beethoven's "Appassionata" Sonata • Brahms's Piano Sonata No 3 • Chopin's Piano Sonata No 2, "Funeral March"

The recording

MITSUKO UCHIDA

⊙ Philips 456 572-2PH + ▣➔

Mitsuko Uchida follows the score's instructions to play quietly, and even quieter still, with great attention, but she's no slave to the minutiae of the music. She allows its poetry to fly freely and creates a quite magical impression. While others may find a stronger sense of foreboding right from the start, she allows the emotion to well up with a powerful sense of the inevitable.

STRING QUINTET
in C (1828)
Perhaps the most sublime chamber work ever written

Schubert's one string quintet is his last chamber work. It is also, by general consent, his finest, composed in 1828 and thus, together with the last three piano sonatas, among the handful of masterpieces he completed during the last months of his life. Amazingly, though a rehearsal of the Quintet took place in October, there is no record of a public performance prior to 1850. Scored for two violins, one viola and two cellos, it has four movements. Words cannot do justice to the sublime beauty of the second (*Adagio*), certainly the most exquisite movement in the whole of Schubert's instrumental music.

If you like this, try: Schubert's "Death and the Maiden" String Quartet • Mozart's string quintets • Brahms's Piano Quintet • Elgar's Piano Quintet

The recording

**HAGEN QUARTET
HEINRCH SCHIFF**

⊙ DG 439 774-2GH + ▣➔

The youthful Hagen Quartet and the hugely experienced Heinrich Schiff combine to wonderful effect. They manage to find a perfect balance between the tragic power of the work and its moment of sublime, poetic beauty. Their control of the work's dynamics from the gentlest of *pianissimos* and the loudest of *fortes* is quite superb.

SCHUBERT ESSENTIALS

Piano Quintet in A, "Trout" (1819)

Schubert dreamt up this lovable work in the beautiful countryside of Steyr – happy melodies and a carefree spirit permeate every bar of this masterpiece of chamber music. It is scored for piano, violin, viola, cello and double bass and is still the only important quintet in the entire repertory that features a part for double bass. The main cause of the Quintet's popularity is a set of five variations on Schubert's own song *Die Forelle* ("The Trout").

Piano music (1822-28)

Moments musicaux (1823-28) - a form that Schubert invented and which describes, as you'd expect, brief musical thoughts; No 3 in F minor is especially popular. *Impromptus* (1828) – these are like short improvisations. There are two sets of four: D899 and D935 – all are, without exception, miniature masterpieces. *Fantasia* in F minor (1828) – a piano duet and a late work whose opening theme (another example of Schubert's "serene melancholy") will take your breath away. Fantasy in C (*Wanderer* Fantasy, 1822) – an extended solo piano work (fiercesomely difficult to play) which begins and ends in heroic style.

Songs

72 of them are settings of poems by Goethe, 47 by Mayrhofer and 46 by Schiller, adorned with Schubert's inexhaustible treasure chest of melody. *An die musik* is a good starting point – "To Music" – a radiant song in praise of music from 1815. *An Sylvia* ("Who is Sylvia") from 1826 is one of the best-known, using a translation of Shakespeare. The most popular, however, is *Ave Maria*; the words are taken from Sir Walter Scott's *The Lady of the Lake*. *Erlkönig* ("The Erl-King") was Schubert's first published song (1821), his Op 1, and is a dramatic setting of Goethe's tale of the father and his dying son riding through night and wind.

SYMPHONY NO 8 "UNFINISHED" (1822)
Unfinished only in length

No one is quite certain why Schubert left his Eighth Symphony unfinished. All we know is that he began its composition in Vienna on October 30, 1822, intending it as a gift to the city of Graz who had elected him an honorary member of the Music Society. What they ended up getting was one movement in B minor, a second in E major and just nine bars of a scherzo. Whatever the reason (and thousands of words have been written in speculation on the subject), this, one of the most beloved of all symphonies, was not heard until 30 years after Schubert's death after its discovery in a pile of other Schubert manuscripts by George Grove and Arthur Sullivan.

113

The recording

ROYAL CONCERTGEBOUW ORCHESTRA / NIKOLAUS HARNONCOURT

⊙ Warner Classics 0927-49813-2 + ⮕

Nikolaus Harnoncourt finds a deep seam of tragedy in this great and wonderfully compressed symphony. Never exaggerated or attention-seeking, Harnoncourt unfolds the work with great sureness and logic. Needless to say, the great Amsterdam orchestra responds with playing of burnished beauty.

If you like this, try: Mendelssohn's Symphony No 5, "Reformation" • Brahms's Symphony No 3 • Tchaikovsky's Symphony No 1 • Elgar's Symphony No 2

WINTERREISE
(1827)
A psychologically profound study in isolation and rejection

The song-cycle *Winterreise* ("Winter Journey") contains 24 songs, and again Schubert turned to the poet of *Die schöne Müllerin*, Wilhlem Müller, though the mood here is more melancholic (Schubert was at a low ebb at the time and probably terminally ill). This psychologically penetrating series of songs traces the aimless journey of a man in a winter landscape – the cold and inhospitable surroundings mirror the poet's inner turmoil and anxiety. He's been rejected in love, and his life has lost its meaning. Müller's powerful verse and Schubert's often desolate music fuse to miraculous effect, at times conjuring up a bitterness that's almost palpable: the way the dogs snarl at this outsider is painful to witness. Contained within this cycle are some of Schubert's greatest songs: "Gute nacht", "Der Lindenbaum", "Die Krähe", and the agonising last song about the hurdy-gurdy man.

The recording

**MARK PADMORE
PAUL LEWIS**

⊙ Harmonia Mundi HMU90 7484 + ⊡➔

A tenor who is singing better than ever and whose voice can convey real pain, here teams up with one of the most thoughtful and poetic pianists of the younger generation. This is a long journey for performers to undertake but these two make it one full of fascinating insights and intriguing colours. There have been many recordings with "concert" pianists and this must now be counted as one of the most successful.

BEN WRIGHT

If you like this, try: Schubert's Die schöne Müllerin
• Schumann's Dichterliebe • Beethoven's An die ferne Geliebte
• Britten's Winter Words

ROBERT SCHUMANN

Born Zwickau 1810 **Died** Endenich 1856

Schumann is a key figure in the Romantic movement; none investigated the Romantic's obsession with feeling and passion quite so thoroughly as him. Schumann died insane, but then some psychologists argue that madness is a necessary attribute of genius.

Though his father, a prosperous bookseller and publisher, encouraged his musical talent, Schumann was persuaded to study law in nearby Leipzig. At the same time, he began piano lessons with his future father-in-law, Friedrich Wieck. In 1829 his elder sister Emilie committed suicide and shortly afterwards his father died suddenly at the age of 53. He persuaded his mother and guardian to allow him to study music with Wieck, determined to become a world-famous virtuoso like Wieck's talented young daughter Clara. In 1832 he permanently injured his right hand by using a mechanical device to help strengthen and lift the middle finger. That was the end of his ambitions as a concert pianist. From about this time he noted unaccountable periods of angst, momentary losses of consciousness and aural hallucinations; he suffered from insomnia and acrophobia and confided in his diary that he was afraid of going mad.

Nevertheless, throughout the 1830s, Schumann's reputation as a composer slowly grew while he also developed his literary activities. In 1834 he co-founded a progressive journal, the *Neue Zeitschrift für Musik*, which fulminated against the vapid salon music of the day. His perceptive writing made him one of the foremost critics of the day. He also translated his journalistic and musical convictions into an association of intimate friends which he named *Davidsbündler*: David against the Philistines – a group that would oppose philistinism in the arts and support passionately all that was new and imaginative. In 1840,

after a lengthy courtship and in the face of violent opposition from Friedrich Wieck, he married Clara. Schumann's career as a composer clearly entered a new stage: that year alone he wrote over 100 songs and in 1841, during the space of only four days, he sketched out his Symphony No 1 in B flat, the *Spring* Symphony. Many other masterful works followed rapidly but, though Clara was intensely ambitious for her husband, the two of them found it hard to balance their two careers. She was far more famous than him.

On a concert tour of Russia in 1844 he found it galling to be introduced as "the husband of Clara Schumann". He resigned from the teaching post Mendelssohn had created for him at his new conservatory in Leipzig and in 1844, the Schumanns moved to Dresden. The great Piano Concerto was composed here, the Second Symphony, and more songs, but from the late 1840s it was clear that Schumann was becoming increasingly unstable.

In 1850 he accepted the post of director of music in Düsseldorf. It proved to be a disaster. Schumann was no conductor. With his inability to communicate and, at times unaware of his surroundings, he was forced to resign. Aural hallucinations were now accompanied by visions of demons and angels and on February 27, 1854 he tried to kill himself by jumping into the Rhine. He was rescued and placed at his own request in an asylum at Endenich near Bonn. Schumann lived on in this unhappy state for a further two years.

PIANO CONCERTO
(1841-45)
A wonderful outpouring of Romantic expression

Schumann's most popular composition and one of the most loved of all piano concertos. Like Grieg, he wrote just one, in the key of A minor. It begins with a single dramatic blow from the orchestra, followed by the piano's downward cascade of chords before the beautiful first theme, recognisable to every German as the *Leben Sie wohl* ("Fare you well") phrase from Schubert's *Wanderer's "Nightsong"*. More than a decade after the concerto's first appearance, the musical Philistines of London indulgently passed off Clara Schumann's performance of this concerto as "praiseworthy efforts…to make her husband's curious rhapsody pass for music".

If you like this, try: Grieg's Piano Concerto • Schumann's Cello Concerto • Rachmaninov's Piano Concerto No 1 • Mendelssohn's Piano Concerto No 1

The recording

**MARIA JOÃO PIRES
CHAMBER ORCHESTRA OF
EUROPE / CLAUDIO ABBADO**
⊙ DG 463 179-2GH + ➡
Maria João Pires mines the poetry of this great concerto with all the imagination and grace we've come to expect of her. Claudio Abbado, a regular and deeply sympathetic partner, is totally attuned to her musical approach and the superb Chamber Orchestra of Europe offer their customary vibrant playing.

FANTASIE
(1838)
Schumann's gift to Liszt, and one of his most passionate piano works

Though Schumann's youthful ambition to be a great piano virtuoso was curtailed in 1832, it did not prevent him from making some of the most important contributions to the literature of the piano, not least this masterpiece which he dedicated to Liszt. Writing to his beloved Clara, Schumann confided: "I do not think I ever wrote anything more impassioned than the first movement. It is a profound lament about you". After this comes a heroic march and then a final movement that has been described as "a pure stream of beatific melody".

If you like this, try: Schumann's Kreisleriana • Schumann's Faschingsschwank aus Wien • Schumann's Piano Sonata No 1 • Liszt's Piano Sonata • Mendelssohn's Variations sérieuses

The recording

SVIATOSLAV RICHTER
⊙ EMI 575233-2 + ➡
The Russian Sviatoslav Richter, one of the keyboard giants of the last century, was a wonderful Schumann pianist. Every phrase not only has great integrity but is beautifully shaped. He homes in on the score's poetry and brings every bar alive. This is a classic performance that no lover of piano music should be without.

SCHUMANN ESSENTIALS

Carnaval (1835)

During a brief departure from his obsession with Clara Wieck, Schumann wrote this much-loved piano masterpiece for Ernestine von Frick. Ernestine lived in the Bohemian town of Asch. In German musical notation, "ASCH" can become musical notes: A, Es (E flat), C and H (B natural). These four notes These four notes (which also happen to correspond to the only musical letters in SCHumAnn's name) provide the theme for *Carnaval*, a succession of character sketches he subtitled "little scenes for the piano on four notes".

Piano Quintet in E flat (1842)

Schumann's most frequently performed chamber work, composed for string quartet and piano, was influential in providing the inspiration for later works of the same ilk by Brahms, Dvořák and Franck. It was written in a white-hot burst of creativity in September 1842. Schumann dedicated it to Clara who was to have been the pianist at its first performance. At the last moment she fell ill, her place taken by Mendelssohn who played the difficult piano part at sight.

Symphony No 1 in B flat ('Spring') (1841)

Schumann's First Symphony was sketched in the remarkably short time of four days at the end of January 1841; all four movements were completed by February 20. It was inspired by a poem by the obscure Adolph Böttger but, as Schumann himself admitted, it was "the season in which the Symphony originated [that] has influenced its form and made it what it is". From this you can gather that you're in for a genial, energetic and immediately attractive work bursting with Mendelssohnian high spirits and melodic inspiration. The Symphony was dedicated to Friedrich August, King of Saxony; the first performance was conducted by Mendelssohn.

SIM CANETTY-CLARKE

DICHTERLIEBE (1840)
A magical cycle from Schumann's year of song

Three monumental song collections, all composed in 1840 when his marriage to Clara was a certainty, contain a plethora of miniature masterpieces. These are: *Liederkreis*, Op 24 ("Song cycle"), *Frauenliebe und -Leben*, Op 42 ("Woman's Life and Love") and *Dichterliebe*, Op 48 ("A Poet's Love"). The great singers of the world have always counted the latter as among their most treasured possessions. The settings of Heine's poems show what a unique sensitivity Schumann had for a verse text. The piano plays as important a role as the voice, commenting on and defining the character and emotional content and sometimes given proportionately-long introductory and concluding passages, raising the art of German song to new heights.

117

The recording

GERALD FINLEY
JULIUS DRAKE

⊙ Hyperion CDA67676 + ▶

Gerald Finley's beautiful bass-baritone voice is heard here in its absolute prime – rich, expressive and capable of conveying remarkable gradations of colour and emotion. Partnered by the ever-sensitive Julius Drake, Finley gives a glorious performance of this great cycle – one that is a total joy in every bar. A worthy winner of a *Gramophone* Award this year.

If you like this, try: Schumann's Liederkreis • Brahms's Vier ernste Gesänge • Schubert's Die schöne Müllerin • Mahler's Lieder eines fahrenden Gesellen

DMITRI SHOSTAKOVICH

Born St Petersburg 1906 **Died** Moscow 1975

Shostakovich at his best is among the most vital and original of 20th-century composers in music notable for rapid exchange of emotional extremes (very Russian) from the sublime to the banal, sarcastic wit to brooding melancholy. He uses modern compositional techniques but never abandons tonality.

While Prokofiev and Stravinsky had grown up under the Tsars, Shostakovich was the first and greatest composer to emerge from Communism. His first music lessons came from his mother, a professional pianist, but it was Glazunov who took him under his wing when he entered the St Petersburg Conservatory at the age of 13. His graduation composition was his First Symphony, a work which made him internationally known aged 20. As a child of the revolution, Shostakovich believed it was the duty of an artist to serve the state.

Yet his next venture, the satirical opera *The Nose*, was attacked by the arbiters of Soviet musical taste as "bourgeois decadence". The same year, his Third Symphony, subtitled *May First*, was criticised as being no more than "a formal gesture of proletarian solidarity". This was nothing compared to the reaction to his opera *Lady Macbeth of the Mtsensk District* (1934) which shocked puritan officialdom. After the opera's Moscow production, *Pravda* published an article headed "Chaos instead of Music" accusing Shostakovich of creating "a bedlam of noise", "a confused stream of sounds" and "petty bourgeois sensationalism".

Shostakovich apologised for his errors, said he would try to do better (even though he thought he had been) and would henceforth write music that fell in line with "socialist realism" (whatever that meant). After his next stage work was also condemned by *Pravda*,

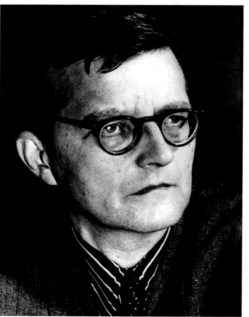

Shostakovich abandoned the theatre and from 1938 to 1955 wrote chiefly symphonies and string quartets.

His Fourth Symphony was withdrawn before its first performance but the Fifth Symphony (1937) let him in from the cold. During the War, he served as a fire-fighter during the siege of Leningrad before being flown to the temporary Soviet capital Kuibishev to complete his Seventh Symphony, *Leningrad*, inspired by the event. Performances in every Allied country led to its composer becoming a kind of artistic war hero.

Even this esteem was not enough to save Shostakovich from being denounced in the famous edict of 1948 when he, along with Prokofiev and other prominent Russian composers, were accused of "formalism" and "anti-people art". He defended himself with some dignity and wrote only film scores and patriotic music until after Stalin's death in 1953. Symphonies Nos 9, 10 and 11 created little interest, No 12 (dedicated to the memory of Lenin) a little more, but with his Symphony No 13, Shostakovich again met with official criticism, this time from the Communist Party chairman Nikita Khruschev who complained about the text of the choral part. Shostakovich's final two symphonies passed the political quality test without controversy. In the '60s, restrictions were slackened somewhat. Shostakovich was left more or less in peace to compose as he wished, and many of the works previously condemned were now given a clean bill of health. It is a tragic irony that his own health then began to deteriorate.

SHOSTAKOVICH ESSENTIALS

Symphony No 5 in D minor (1937)

In early 1936, Stalin expressed his outrage at Shostakovich's opera *Lady Macbeth of Mtsensk* and the composer suddenly found himself out of public favour and in fear for his life. The Fifth Symphony, subtitled "A Soviet Artist's Practical Creative Reply to Just Criticism", was Shostakovich's tightrope response, a work that would appease the Soviet authorities while remaining true to his musical ideals. It was premiered in November 1937 to public and critical acclaim and is by far the most frequently heard of all his 15 symphonies. Its four movements are written in striking contrast to each other – a dramatic and powerful opening, a waltz-like *scherzo*, a profoundly-felt slow movement and a march-like finale which ends in a blaze of brass and timpani.

Piano Quintet (1940)

One of Shostakovich's finest works, the Quintet was premiered on November 23, 1940 at the Moscow Festival of Soviet Music and was awarded the Stalin Prize of 100,000 roubles. It opens with a Prelude and Fugue, followed by an impish *scherzo* and a concluding *Intermezzo* of infectious gaiety.

24 Preludes and Fugues (1950-51)

Tatyana Nikolayeva (1924-93) won first prize in the 1950 Bach Competition in Leipzig. Shostakovich happened to be on the jury and was so impressed by her performances of Bach's preludes and fugues that he set about writing a set of his own for the pianist. She would telephone him every day during the period of composition, visiting his home to try it out. She gave the first performance of the complete cycle in Leningrad in 1952, Shostakovich's most important contribution to piano literature.

SYMPHONY NO 10
(1953)
Shostakovich reflecting on a post-Stalin world?

For many, this is Shostakovich's finest achievement. Its odd-number movements are dark and melancholy, the two even-number movements upbeat and ebullient. The motif for the work is the compsoer's personal musical monogram – the notes D, E flat, C and B natural correspond to D, Es [S], C, H in German notation – D-S-C-H). The scherzo is said to be a portrait of Stalin while the slow (third) movement opens with a folk-song in the strings followed by a nocturne-like solo for horn over *pizzicato* strings. The finale recalls material from the previous three. Shostakovich's Tenth was written just after the death of Stalin, perhaps reflecting the dark ages that had passed and the optimism for a better future.

The recording

BERLIN PHILHARMONIC ORCHESTRA / HERBERT VON KARAJAN

⊙ DG 477 5909GOR + ▣➔

This is one of Karajan's greatest recordings: it was a work he performed in Moscow in the presence of its composer – Shostakovich was apparently deeply moved by the concert. Karajan, perhaps surprisingly given the image that adheres to him, was perfectly attuned to this music and the world it emerged from. He'd

lived through the Second World War and the experience made a huge impression on him – and it comes across powerfully in this fine performance.

If you like this, try: Shostakovich's Symphony No 8 • Shostakovich's Cello Concerto No 2 • Prokofiev's Symphony No 6 • Britten's Sinfonia da requiem

CONCERTO FOR PIANO, TRUMPET AND STRINGS (1933)

Shostakovich revealing his talent for light-hearted music

Described variously as "fun-poking and mighty refreshing", "without exaggeration…disagreeable music" and sounding as if "it might have been written by a schoolboy with his cap set rakishly on the back of his head", Shostakovich's concerto is both entertaining and exhilarating. The trumpet part is extensive, using both its bravura and lyrical capabilities to the full in music that has echoes of Poulenc, Prokofiev and even Rachmaninov. The concerto's four short movements end with a coruscating finale, including a piano cadenza inspired by Beethoven's rondo "Rage over a lost penny". There is a splendid recording of the composer himself as soloist in the work.

120

The recording

DMITRI ALEXEEV; PHILIP JONES; ENGLISH CHAMBER ORCHESTRA / JERZY MAKSYMIUK

⊙ Classics for Pleasure 382234-2 + ⤷
Dmitri Alexeev is a wonderfully lively soloist who relishes the jazzy rhythms as much as the work's more languid moments. With a star trumpeter as a companion, and the ECO on top form under a conductor really attuned to the idiom of this music, you have a winner. And the couplings of the Second Piano Concerto and the suite from the film score *The Unforgettable Year 1919* make it simply unmissable.

STEVE RAPPORT

If you like this, try: Shostakovich's Piano Concerto No 2
• Shostakovich's Jazz Suites • Prokofiev's Piano Concerto No 2
• Martinů's La revue de cuisine • Bernstein's Age of Anxiety

JEAN SIBELIUS

Born Hämeenlinna 1865

Died Järvenpää 1957

Sibelius is a national icon. "He is Finland in music; and he is Finnish music," observed one critic. An austere grandeur, an icy, brooding quality impels admiration and inspires awe, for here in music is the bleak Nordic landscape at the mercy of the unforgiving elements.

After early piano and violin lessons, the law drew him briefly but music quickly took over. Encouraged by Busoni, who was on the staff of the Music Academy at Helsinki, in 1889 Sibelius went off to Berlin for further study, then to Vienna as a pupil of Karl Goldmark. On his return to Finland in 1891 he produced his first major composition, the *Kullervo* Symphony based on an episode from the great Finnish epic poem *Kalevala*. Overnight, this ambitious score established him as the country's most important composer.

Finnish mythology had a profound effect on him and he formed the ideal of creating music that resonated with his country's ancient legends and so reflect the spirit and unique culture of his people. Works like *En Saga*, *The Swan of Tuonela* and his First Symphony had a tremendous impact. Above all, it was *Finlandia*, an overtly patriotic orchestral work, which identified him with the growing nationalist movement.

A grant from the enlightened Finnish Senate enabled him to give up all other work so that he could concentrate entirely on composing. This was not enough to keep him out of debt and he and his wife were beset with money worries all through the 1890s to the end of the First World War. Ironically, he sold one of his most popular compositions, the little salon *Valse triste* to his publishers for 300 marks – it made them a fortune. He was also a heavy drinker with a fondness for beer and cognac as well as fine cigars.

In 1901 a disease of the ear threatened to make him totally deaf – it was successfully treated – and seven years later he had to undergo 13 throat operations to remove a malignant growth, at first diagnosed as cancer. His music during this period (including the *Valse triste* and the melancholy Fourth Symphony) reflect his morbid frame of mind at the time.

By the outbreak of War, honours were being heaped upon him as he travelled all over Europe and even to America to conduct his music. The War not only cut off his foreign visits and royalties but heralded the complete stop to all creative activity. Apart from some trivial (and not very good) piano music, only the Fifth Symphony was composed during the conflict, completed in time for his 50th birthday celebrations. Finland proclaimed its independence after the October Revolution and was plunged into a civil war after a coup d'état by the Red Guards. Sibelius's brother was murdered and he himself was forced to flee the Villa Ainola, which since 1904 had been his home in Järvenpää, to the north of Helsinki.

After the war he composed his Sixth and Seventh Symphonies, the symphonic poem *Tapiola* and the incidental music to a production of *The Tempest*. He travelled, he toured, he conducted, but his last-known work was completed in 1931. For the last 26 years of his life Sibelius did not publish another note. Following the Second World War he was a virtual recluse. He was 91 when he died of a cerebral haemorrhage.

121

VIOLIN CONCERTO

(1903 rev 1905)

One of the cornerstones of the violinist's repertoire

The violin was Sibelius's first study instrument and at one time he entertained thoughts of becoming a soloist (as late as 1891 he auditioned for the strings of the Vienna Philharmonic). You can call this "the Sibelius Concerto" because this is the only concerto he wrote for any instrument. It is one of the cornerstones of the violinist's repertoire and all the great artists have risen to its challenge, though it took over 30 years and a recording by the legendary Jascha Heifetz before this happened. Not an easy work to play, the concerto has three movements: the first is one of romantic ardour, the second poignant and poetic, the last passionate and impulsive with enormous rhythmic vitality.

122

The recording

LEONIDAS KAVAKOS; LAHTI SYMPHONY ORCHESTRA / OSMO VÄNSKÄ

⊙ BIS BIS-CD500 + ⯈

This disc offers the fascinating opportunity to hear both versions of Sibelius's marvellous concerto – his first thoughts, and the revised version. Listening to original played with great virtuosity and excellent taste by Leonidas Kavakos and the superb Lahti orchestra is an absorbing experience.

They play splendidly throughout, and the familiar Concerto which was struggling to get out of the

1903-4 version emerges equally safely in their hands. Invaluable.

YANNIS BOURNIAS

If you like this, try: Sibelius's Tapiola • Sibelius's Finlandia • Sibelius's Fifth Symphony • Elgar's Violin Concerto • Lindberg's Violin Concerto

SIBELIUS ESSENTIALS

Karelia Suite (1893)

Karelia is an area in the eastern part of Finland where the inhabitants are said to have a much jollier disposition than their counterparts in the west. This is reflected in some of the most carefree and exuberant music Sibelius ever wrote. The three short orchestral movements that make up the Karelia Suite are: Intermezzo, Ballade and Alla marcia, taken from the incidental music he provided in 1893 for a student theatre production at the University of Viborg.

The Swan of Tuonela (1893, rev 1897 & 1900)

Sibelius explained this exquisite, plaintive work as depicting "Tuonela [the Finnish equivalent of Hades], the Kingdom of Death...surrounded by a broad river of black water and rapid currents, in which the Swan of Tuonela glides in majestic fashion and sings". The story comes from the epic Finnish poem *Kalevala* and the music is the second of a suite in four sections inspired by *Kalevala* entitled *Lemminkainen Legends*. The Swan is portrayed by the cor anglais and is one of the most beautiful solos ever written for the instrument.

Finlandia (1899, rev 1900)

Sibelius's most celebrated work is a tone poem written (in the form we know it today) in 1900. It was originally the fourth movement of a suite entitled *Finland Awakes* composed a year earlier as part of a series of entertainments inaugurated to raise funds to fight Russia's suppression of the press and free speech in Finland. It is said that the one-movement we now call "Finlandia" did more to bring about Finnish independence than any speech, pamphlet or other propaganda.

SYMPHONY NO 5
(1915 rev 1919)
An expression of its creator's great optimism

The mighty Fifth Symphony was written in the second year of the First World War, a period during which Sibelius suffered not only financial but spiritual trials. Profoundly shocked by the conflict, he struggled to express his feelings in the best way he knew how – the symphonic form. Its completion proved, in the words of Karl Ekman, "an expression of its creator's great optimism, gained through suffering; an elevating testimony, in an evil period, to an unshakable faith in the ever-renewing power of life." The first version, premiered in 1915, was withdrawn, heavily re-written and not presented in the form we know today until 1919. The heroic final movement has been described as "Thor swinging his hammer" and it ends with a famous succession of separated, crunching chords (always hard to know which one is the last!)

123

The recording

HALLÉ ORCHESTRA / SIR JOHN BARBIROLLI

⊙ Testament SBT1418

This recording of Sibelius's Fifth Symphony with Barbirolli's beloved Hallé is taken from the 1968 Proms which – in strength of personality and palpable depth of feeling, it has a lot going for it. The opening pages have exactly the right sense of awe-struck wonder and pregnant growth, and in the second movement it's a joy to hear Sibelius's delicious *pizzicato* writing "speak" with such clarity and eloquence. The first half of the finale has vitality and atmosphere in abundance.

Sir John Barbirolli
Sibelius Symphonies Nos.2 & 5
Royal Philharmonic Orchestra · Hallé Orchestra

TESTAMENT

If you like this, try: Sibelius's Symphony No 2 • Mahler's Symphony No 5 • Rachmaninov's Symphony No 2 • Rautavaara's Symphony No 7 "Angel of Light"

RICHARD STRAUSS

Born Munich 1864

Died Garmisch-Partenkirchen 1949

The dramatic power, soaring intensity and grandeur in the operas and tone poems Strauss wrote between 1885 and 1910 has never been equalled. For his remaining 40 years, while certainly not resting on his laurels, he fell back on his extreme technical accomplishment, professional adroitness and sophistication.

Richard Strauss was a *wunderkind* whose father was the leading horn player in Munich. He began piano lessons when he was four and completed his first composition when he was six. His Op 1, a *Festmarsch* for Orchestra written when he was 12, was published in 1880. He very quickly made a name for himself, his technical assurance (if not his style) seemingly pre-formed. It's not everyone that has their first symphony, a violin concerto and a second symphony (played by the New York Philharmonic) all premiered and under their belt by the age of 20.

The decade from 1887 saw a succession of tone poems which made his name throughout the musical word. Now, such masterpieces as *Don Juan, Till Eulenspiegel, Ein Heldenleben Also Sprach Zarathustra* and *Don Quixote* are as much a part of basic orchestral repertoire as Beethoven's symphonies but when they were first heard the critics could not find enough adjectives with which to condemn them. By the turn of the century Strauss was recognised not only among the most important and provocative composers of the time but in the front rank of great conductors. In 1898 he was given one of the most important musical posts in the world – the conductorship of the Berlin Philharmonic which he retained for a dozen years. Using his immense influence he introduced a system by which, for the first time, German composers would receive a royalty from every performance of their work by a major orchestra or opera house. Concurrent with

the tone poems were Strauss's operas. *Guntram* (1894) and *Feuersnot* (1901) were failures (the lead soprano in *Guntram* was Pauline de Ahna; she married Strauss in September 1894, remaining with him, despite a stormy relationship, until the end of his life, dying only months after him).

In 1900 he met the poet Hugo von Hofmannsthal, a librettist who was to have a profound effect on his career in the theatre. Their collaboration began with *Salome*, premiered in 1905, followed by *Elektra* in 1909. These managed to provoke the same hearty opprobrium as the tone poems. As if by way of concession their next venture, *Der Rosenkavalier* could not have been more different. It remains among the most cherished of all operas.

Strauss's behaviour during the 1930s and '40s is not easy to excuse. True he spoke out against the regime when he insisted on working with the Jewish librettist Stefan Zweig, but when asked why he did not leave the country, Strauss reportedly replied: "Germany had 56 opera houses; the United States had two. It would have reduced my income." He and his wife went to live in Switzerland for most of the Second World War but returned to their villa in the Bavarian Alps after the conflict. He was cleared of Nazi affiliations in 1948, after facing a special court in Munich. So revered was he by the musical world that he was feted during his visit to London in 1947 and his 85 birthday was celebrated world-wide, just a few months before he died.

STRAUSS ESSENTIALS

Don Juan (1888)

This is the first of Strauss's famous "tone poems" (the first that made an impression, that is, for he had written an earlier one called *Macbeth*). Its musical story is based on the celebrated, insatiable lover and his search for the perfect woman. Strauss threw aside all the influences that had shaped his music thus far (he was only 24 at the time) writing in a daring and bombastic way which many found offensive – the ardent, passionate nature of the music created a storm of controversy when it was first performed. It made Strauss's name.

Der Rosenkavalier (1911)

To many people "The Cavalier of the Rose" is the last great Romantic opera. It is certainly the most popular German opera of the 20th century. Strauss's two earlier operas, *Salome* and *Elektra*, were written in a harsh, dissonant musical language, but for this he reverted to lush romantic writing that pulls at the heart strings. Set in 18th-century Vienna, it tells the story of the love between the Princess von Werdenberg (known as the Marschallin), her young suitor Octavian and his beloved Sophie. The Act 3 vocal climax is one of the most ravishing passages in all opera.

Songs (1885-1948)

Because of the fame of his operas and tone poems, Strauss the songwriter is often overlooked. He composed more than 135, the greatest written before he was 30. These Eight Songs (Op 10) from 1885 include *Zueignung* ("Dedication"), *Die Nacht* ("The Night") and Allerseelen ("All Soul's Day"), are all miniature masterpieces. From his Six Songs (Op 17) of 1885 comes the lovely *Ständchen* ("Serenade") while the Four Songs (Op 27) of 1894 has *Cäcilie* and *Morgen* ("Tomorrow") – but dip in anywhere and you'll find treasure.

TILL EULENSPIEGEL'S MERRY PRANKS (1895)

Strauss shows off his prowess as a master of the orchestra

"Till Owlglass" is how you would translate the name of this character in German legend, a cheat and a rogue, found in the folklore of every country (for example, in Russia he is Ivan the Fool, in Italy he is Lochinello). In this tone poem, Strauss tells Till's story from his early pranks and practical jokes, Till causing mischief and mayhem, Till in love, Till rejected, to Till caught, tried and hanged. In the legend, he escapes the gallows but Strauss has him swing…though the cheeky little pay-off from the orchestra makes you wonder whether he really died after all. It's all there in the music painted with Strauss's ingenious and colourful orchestration.

125

The recording

BERLIN PHILHARMONIC ORCHESTRA / HERBERT VON KARAJAN

⊙ DG 447 441-2GOR + ▷

Karajan was always a great conductor of comic operas and this compact tone-poem certainly calls for a comic touch. The playing of the great Berlin Phil is magnificent, embracing the myriad colours and moods of this little gem. You also get one of the greatest recordings of Strauss's *Also sprach Zarathustra* ever made.

If you like this, try: Strauss's Don Juan • Strauss's Le bourgeois gentilhomme • Dukas's Sorcerer's Apprentice • Elgar's Falstaff • Britten's La boutique fantasque

FOUR LAST SONGS
(1948)

Strauss bids farewell to the soprano voice with these four great songs

After Strauss completed his last opera, *Capriccio*, in 1941, he declared "From now on it will all be for harps". In fact, far from hanging up his pen after a creative period of six decades, he turned out a series of autumnal masterpieces topped by these Four Last Songs begun early in 1947 and completed less than a fortnight after his 84th birthday. All were conceived for the orchestra as much as the voice: the first three end with a solo passage for the French horn, an instrument as close to Strauss's heart as the soprano voice for which they were written; all are written in a mood of accepting, calm serenity. The first to be composed was the last song in the published set: "At Sunset" with words by Eichendorff; the other three have words by Hermann Hesse. After a lifetime of writing for the soprano voice (the voice-type of his wife Pauline) he signed off gloriously with these songs.

The recording

**SOILE ISOKOSKI
BERLIN RADIO SYMPHONY
ORCHESTRA / MAREK JANOWSKI**

⊙ Ondine ODE982-2 + ↦

The Finnish soprano Soile Isokoski, one of the great Strauss singers of our time, enters the crowded field of *Four Last Songs* recordings, and succeeds triumphantly. Her voice soars effortlessly over the orchestra (beautifully handled by Marek Janowski), and she spins the long lines out without any apparent

concern for breathing! Her pure soprano voice can smile when necessary, but it also conveys the wonderful sense of acceptance that life will draw peacefully to a close after a long and happy life.

HEIKKI TUULI

If you like this, try: Strauss's Drei Hymnen • Strauss's Capriccio • Ravel's Shéhérazade • Berlioz's Les nuits d'été • Barber's Knoxville: Summer of 1915

STRAVINSKY

From 1910 to 1945, Stravinsky was the single strongest influence on contemporary music. His early ballets alone were enough to secure his place among the greats. The intellectual rigour of his second, neo-classical period and the third, serial period has led to his music being more respected than loved.

Stravinsky's father had sent his son to study law at St Petersburg University, but after his death in 1902 Igor began taking lessons in orchestration from Rimsky-Korsakov. To celebrate the wedding of Rimsky-Korsakov's daughter, Stravinsky (1882-1971) wrote an orchestral fantasy called *Feu d'artifice* (Fireworks). The work was given in a concert in St Petersburg in 1909. In the audience was Serge Diaghilev the ballet impresario, who commissioned *The Firebird* (which made Stravinsky famous overnight), *Petrushka* and *The Rite of Spring*.

After the revolution of 1917 Stravinsky opted for voluntary exile in Paris. *Pulcinella* (1920) marked the beginning of a second stage in his musical development. With the Second World War inevitable, Stravinsky accepted an invitation from Harvard University to hold the chair of Professor of Poetry and moved to America. In 1948 he agreed to return to the theatre, and wrote *The Rake's Progress*. While working on this he was introduced to the music of Schoenberg and the Second Viennese School and began to cautiously experiment with the technique. Thus began the third period of his development, producing his first composition in the new form at the age of 75, *Agon* (1957).

In 1962, just before his 80th birthday, Stravinsky made a triumphant return to Russia. Throughout the decade he was feted as few other musicians in history, universally acknowledged as the greatest living composer. He died in New York in 1971 and was buried on the Venetian island of San Michele.

THE RITE OF SPRING
(1913)
The cause of such high emotion was the extraordinary music

If the sophisticated pre-First World War audience of Paris thought they had heard modern Russian music in Stravinsky's *The Firebird* and *Petrushka*, nothing could have prepared them for *Le Sacre du Printemps* (The Rite of Spring), subtitled "Scenes of Pagan Russia". Its premiere on the night of May 29, 1913 caused a riot. The cause of such high emotion was the extraordinary music that Stravinsky had dreamt up. To some people it was the work of a madman, a violent wrench from every musical tradition that had gone before. Stravinsky introduced weird and discordant effects, rapid and frequent changes of tempo and unusual combinations of instruments. Less than 30 years later, Stravinsky's score had become so much part of the standard repertoire that it was included in Walt Disney's 1940 film *Fantasia*.

127

The recording

CITY OF BIRMINGHAM SYMPHONY ORCHESTRA / SIR SIMON RATTLE

⊙ EMI 749636-2 +

A refreshingly thoughtful, immaculately honed *Rite* from Rattle. Rhythm and ensemble are consistently tight; nor is there any lack of primitivistic fervour. Rattle sees the work as a whole, without striving for a spurious symphonic integration, and there's never for a moment any hint of a routine reading of what's now a classic of the modern orchestral repertoire.

If you like this, try: Stravinsky's The Firebird
• Stravinsky's Petrushka • Ravel's Daphnis et Chloé
• Stravinsky's The Rake's Progress

Sir Simon Rattle *Conductor*
From Birmingham to Berlin,
Rattle's stupendous musicianship
has taken him a long way. We
feature him in Debussy (page 33)
and Stravinsky (page 127)

PHOTO • MAT HENNEK/EMI ARCHIVES

TALLIS

Tallis (c1505-85) served four Tudor monarchs all of whom required him to adopt different attitudes to religious affairs. Rather than inhibiting him, these changes seem to inspire his creative impetus.

Little is known of Tallis's early life. Born around 1505, he went on to hold a succession of posts as organist, most notably at Waltham Abbey in Essex (until the dissolution of the monasteries in 1540) before joining the Gentlemen of the Chapel Royal from about 1543. He remained there for the rest of his life, serving under Henry VIII, Edward VI, Mary and Elizabeth I. In 1572, William Byrd (40 years his junior) joined Tallis in the Chapel Royal, forming one of music's earliest great partnerships: they became joint organists of the Chapel and, in 1575, were granted the sole right to print music in England. Their first publication was a joint venture – a volume of *Cantiones sacrae* to which each contributed 17 motets. Tallis died in 1585, his epitaph reading: "As he did live, so also did he die, in mild and happy sort, (O! happy man)".

Most of Tallis's music is, not surprisingly, for the church and his historic importance is in being one of the first composers to write for the Anglican service, the composer who bridged the transition from the Roman Rite. Though most of the texts Tallis set are in Latin, after Queen Mary's reign he adapted to Thomas Cranmer's English and his insistence on a "playn and distincte note for every sillable".

Tallis composed in the whole range of styles and forms then in use. We can marvel at his handling of choral sonority and grand polyphonic textures as well as in the simplicity of four-part hymn tunes. The one known as *Tallis's Canon* is still used for the evening hymn "Glory to thee, my God, this night". It first appeared in Archbishop Parker's Psalter in which can also be found the tune on which Vaughan Williams based his *Fantasia on a Theme of Thomas Tallis*.

SPEM IN ALIUM
(1570)
Sing and Glorify

Spem in alium nunquam habui ("In no other is my hope" or, in its English setting, "Sing and Glorify Heaven's High Majesty") is a 40-part motet and is Tallis's masterpiece. The text is adapted from the Book of Judith. Tallis asks for five (unaccompanied) choirs, each of eight voices, to enter one after the other, their independent vocal lines gradually building in volume and complexity in one sustained, magisterial hymn of praise. What makes this remarkable even today is that for some considerable part of the work, the 40 different voices join together to sing 40 completely different vocal lines simultaneously. Possibly written for the 40th birthday of Queen Elizabeth, the work's contrapuntal ingenuity and technical assurance make it an overwhelming experience to hear.

129

The recording

MAGNIFICAT / PHILIP CAVE
⊙ Linn Records CKD233 + ➡
Demonstration-quality openness and balance makes this quite spacious version one to treasure. Lots of young British voices, many of them familiar names from other well-established choral groups, bring an unchurchy, dynamic panorama to Tallis's elaborate testament of faith – *My hope is founded in the Lord* – and demonstration of compositional skill.

If you like this, try: Tallis's Lamentations of Jeremiah • Taverner's Missa Gloria tibi Trinitas • Allegri's Miserere mei • Vaughan Williams's Fantasia on a Theme of Thomas Tallis

YAMAHA

A century of making music distilled into our ultimate Hi-Fi:
it could only be Yamaha

CD-S2000 Compact Disc Player

A-S2000 Intergrated Amp

Soavo-1

Yamaha began its quest for sound superiority over 100 years ago - rather earlier than most of our hi-fi competitors.
Since 1887 we've turned our attentions to all manner of musical instruments and professional audio equipment, but never lost sight of our original driving force - the creation and delivery of beautiful, natural sound.
You'll hear the difference when you choose Yamaha for your home.
Discover more at hifi.yamaha-europe.com

 **YAMAHA**

 **av·hi-fi**

Powered by music

PETER ILYICH TCHAIKOVSKY

Born Votkinsk 1840 **Died** St Petersburg 1893

Tchaikovsky is the most popular of all Russian composers, his music combining some nationalist elements with a more cosmopolitan view, but it is music that could only have been written by a Russian. In every genre he shows himself to be one of the greatest melodic fountains who ever lived.

Tchaikovsky was a comparatively late starter among the great composers: he learnt the piano as a boy and when the family moved to St Petersburg in 1850 it was decided that he should read law. Only in his 20s did he begin to make something of his musical gifts.

The decisive factor was the founding of what would become the St Petersburg Conservatory in 1862 by Anton Rubinstein. Tchaikovsky followed his teacher Nicholas Zaremba to the Conservatory and the following year resigned his post as a civil servant to become a full-time musician. Only two years later, Rubinstein's brother Nicholas invited Tchaikovsky to teach harmony at the Moscow Conservatory.

While his first large-scale compositions began to emerge (Symphony No 1, "Winter Dreams" among them) various nervous disorders began to manifest themselves, but his career progressed in an untroubled way for the next few years. Then came a series of crises. Late in 1874 he finished his Piano Concerto No 1 and played it through to Nicholas Rubinstein to whom he had dedicated the work. Rubinstein denounced it as ugly and unplayable. Tchaikovsky was flung into a morbid depression by this and the initial failure of his ballet *Swan Lake*. He tired of his work at the Conservatory, he had financial problems and, nagging away at the back of his mind, was the guilt attached to his homosexuality. In 1877 he married one of his pupils, separating from her nine weeks later and attempting suicide. Providentially, at this time he

found a patron in the person of a wealthy and cultured widow, Nadezhda von Meck, whose yearly allowance allowed him to devote himself full-time to composition. His Fourth Symphony, the opera *Eugene Onegin*, and the Violin Concerto were but three of the works written shortly after Tchaikovsky had been given financial security. For the next 13 years, this extraordinary relationship continued, one of the conditions for her generous subsidy being that they should never meet. The initial burst of unqualified masterpieces was followed by an uneven period but by 1880 he was famous and respected. Then, between 1881 and 1888 he dried up.

Inspiration returned in 1888 with the Fifth Symphony, the government settled an annual pension on him and he made an extensive tour of Europe conducting his works to enormous acclaim. In 1890 Nadezhda von Meck suddenly broke off the relationship with Tchaikovsky for reasons which have never been fully explained. It left Tchaikovsky deeply wounded. After a triumphant tour of the United States in 1891 during which he was profoundly homesick, he returned home to start work on his Sixth Symphony.

In June 1893 he travelled to Cambridge to receive an Honorary Doctorate of Music. In October, he conducted the premiere of the "Pathétique" (it was coolly received). On November 2 he drank a glassful of unboiled tap water and died four days later. Whether it was an accident or deliberate, whether he died from cholera-infected water or committed suicide by poison remains unresolved and a highly contentious issue.

PIANO CONCERTO NO 1
(1875 rev 1879 & 1889)
The world's most played and recorded piano concerto

It opens with a majestic theme from the orchestra accompanied by dynamic chords from the piano. It's among the most arresting passages from any concerto but, after an immediate repeat, is never heard again. For the main body of the first movement Tchaikovsky uses a folk-like tune and a tender melody for French horns and woodwinds. The slow movement's elegiac theme is interrupted by a glittering scherzo-waltz, while the finale features a Russian dance and a lyrical song which becomes the overwhelming climax of the concerto. After denouncing the work at the first performance Nicholas Rubinstein relented and admitted his error by performing it brilliantly at the Paris Exhibition of 1878.

If you like this, try: Liszt's Piano Concerto No 2 • Brahms's Piano Concerto No 2 • Tchaikovsky's Violin Concerto • Rachmaninov's Piano Concerto No 3

The recording

MARTHA ARGERICH
BERLIN PHILHARMONIC
ORCHESTRA / CLAUDIO
ABBADO

⊙ DG 449 816-2GH + ▷

Right from the first orchestral fanfare you just know that this is going to be a very special performance indeed. And as soon as Argerich starts to play, the sparks fly. Her colossal technique, the playing of the Berlin Phil and Abbado's flair and imagination (not to mention his very evidemnt

rapport with his soloist) make this a terrific recording.

THE NUTCRACKER
(1892)
A ballet that explodes with favourite melodies

On Christmas Eve a little girl dreams that the gift of a household nutcracker doll comes to life. She defends it in battle against the Mouse King and his cohorts and, when it changes into a handsome prince, visits the enchanting world of the Sugar Plum Fairy. The ballet is based on ETA Hoffman's fairy tale The Nutcracker and the Mouse King and inspired Tchaikovsky to write some of his most captivating music, without a hint of his characteristic melancholy. The concert suite from the full score is universally popular containing the "Miniature Overture", "Dance of the Sugar Plum Fairy" and "Waltz of the Flowers".

If you like this, try: Tchaikovsky's The Sleeping Beauty • Tchaikovsky's Swan Lake • Delibes's Coppélia • Prokofiev's Cinderella • Shostakovich's The Golden Age

The recording

LONDON SYMPHONY
ORCHESTRA / SIR CHARLES
MACKERRAS

⊙ Telarc CD80140 + ▷

Beautifully recorded (in Watford Town Hall) as you might expect from a company that places great sound high on its list of priorities, this is a Nutcracker full of detail, poetry and elegance. The LSO is the perfect ensemble for this music, playing with stunning clarity and warmth. Mackerras conducts

with a lot of charm and wit. A joy from start to finish.

TCHAIKOVSKY ESSENTIALS

Romeo and Juliet – Fantasy Overture (1869)

Romeo and Juliet is not an overture in the usual sense – it is not a curtain raiser for an opera, for example – but a descriptive concert piece, the "fantasy" element of the title referring to the music's freedom of form. It doesn't follow the play but incidents in the drama are easy to spot: the religious chant for clarinets and bassoons which opens the work represents Friar Lawrence; the turbulent passage which follows paints the feud between the Montagues and Capulets. Then there's the rapturous, poignant lover's theme for Romeo and Juliet, clearly written from the heart – Tchaikovsky composed it after he had been jilted by the beautiful singer Désirée Artôt.

Violin Concerto (1878)

One of the four big violin concertos that every soloist has in their repertoire, the Tchaikovsky is more lyrical and in a lighter vein than the piano concertos. It was dedicated to the legendary violin teacher Leopold Auer who pronounced it unplayable. It took four years before it was heard in public (Vienna, 1881) where, though hard to believe now, it was savaged by the critics. Throughout the work, Tchaikovsky uses Russian-sounding themes.

Eugene Onegin (1879)

Based on Pushkin's poem, *Eugene Onegin* is set in St Petersburg in about 1815 and tells the story of the love that the young, gauche Tatiana feels for the elegant Onegin. He rejects her, then, six years later, he encounters a very different Tatiana, now the radiant and sophisticated wife of a retired general, and falls head over heels for her. Tatiana struggles with her emotions but finally rejects Onegin. It is an intimate work more concerned with poetry and psychological insights than theatrical effects. The highlight is the Letter Scene from Act 1.

SYMPHONY NO 6 "PATHÉTIQUE" (1893)
A magical cycle from Schumann's year of song

The *Pathétique* is a programme-symphony. Exactly what programme, Tchaikovsky teasingly chose not to divulge. "Let them puzzle their heads over it," he wrote. "The programme is subjective through and through, and during my journey I often wept bitterly while composing it in my head." Whatever the message, its final movement is surely the most pessimistic utterance in all music. Among many points of interest along the way are the quote in the first movement from the Russian requiem service "And rest him with the Saints", the waltz-which-isn't-a-waltz of the second, and the too-confidant march of the third movement before the total resignation of the last. The whole work is proof that Tchaikovsky was happiest when he was sad, viewing his sorrows with detachment and encapsulating them in music of the utmost beauty.

133

The recording

RUSSIAN NATIONAL ORCHESTRA / MIKHAIL PLETNEV

⊙ Virgin Classics 561636-2 + ⮕

To make this recording Virgin Classics flew the entire orchestra to London for the sessions: such extravagence paid off because this is one of the most powerful recorded perfomances for many years. This superb Russian orchestra plays at white heat with whip-crack chords, and a depth of sound from the strings that seems to dig deep into the very soul of Old Russia. Listen to this and stay dry eyed? Impossible!

If you like this, try: Tchaikovsky's Symphony No 5 • Bruckner's Symphony No 9 • Mahler's Symphony No 9 • Shostakovich's Symphony No 8

GRAMOPHONE ARCHIVE

923 TO TODAY - EXPLORE EVERY ISSUE OF THE WORLD'S GREATEST CLASSICAL MUSIC MAGAZINE

www.gramophone.net

★ Gramophone Archive allows you to search 85 years of the finest writing on recorded classical music, for free!

★ A comprehensive search facility allows you to home in on specific periods or topics and search for reviews or articles.

★ Now, you need never consider an album purchase without first consulting the leading writers on classical recordings since 1923!

REGISTER TODAY AT WWW.GRAMOPHONE.NET AND JOIN THE WORLD'S LARGEST CLASSICAL MUSIC ARCHIVE!

RALPH VAUGHAN WILLIAMS

Born Down Ampney 1872 **Died** London 1958

**'The art of music above all other arts,' wrote Vaughan Williams, 'is
the expression of the soul of the nation'. His best music transcends
the folk music idiom (as all great nationalist music does) and is
infused with the mysticism and poetry that were so important to him.**

Ralph (pronounced "Rayf") Vaughan Williams was related to a distinguished family of lawyers on his father's side and to both Charles Darwin and Josiah Wedgewood on his mother's. He was brought up in the home of his maternal grandfather in Surrey, after his clergyman father died young. His music studies were nothing if not protracted – he was fortunate in having a private income – for after the Royal College of Music he took a Mus B and BA at Trinity, Cambridge, returned to the Royal College for lessons with Stanford, took off for Berlin for further study with Max Bruch and in 1908, at the age of 36, went to Ravel in Paris for (as he put it) "a little French polish".

After all this schooling in conservative English and German construction, and modern French orchestral technique, Vaughan Williams emerged as an adventurous, unmistakably English composer. His discovery in the early 1900s of English folk song helped focus his distinctive voice. The cataloguing and research that "VW" and his friend Gustav Holst undertook in this area was of considerable cultural significance. Before this, his early works sound like any one of a dozen accomplished composers writing at the turn of the century; afterwards, his music took on a different character. Apart from war service (for which he volunteered, although over 40), Vaughan Williams devoted the rest of his long life to composition, teaching and conducting. Musicologists analyse how Vaughan Williams achieved this "Englishness" by examining his use of modern harmony, parallel triadic progressions, modal counterpoint, polytonality and such like. Music lovers simply hear that hard-to-define-yet-unmistakeable English sound. None but an Englishman could have written the *Fantasia on a theme of Thomas Tallis*, the *Fantasia on Greensleeves*, *The Lark Ascending* or the *Serenade to Music*. Down Ampney, the Cotswold village of his birth, is also the hymn tune to which we sing "Come down, O Love Divine". That, the tune *Sine nomine* ("For all the saints"), *Monks Gate* (the folk tune he used to set the words "Who would true valour see") and his arrangement of the *Old 100th Psalm Tune* ("All people that on earth do dwell") may be his most performed music.

Vaughan Williams worked on into old age with undiminished creative powers. His Eighth Symphony appeared in 1955 (the score includes parts for vibraphone and xylophone) while his Ninth, composed at the age of 85, uses a trio of saxophones. After his wife's death in 1951, he married the poet and librettist Ursula Wood at the age of 80 and moved from his home of many years (The White Gates, near Dorking in Surrey) to a house in London's Regent Park. He was a familiar sight at the capital's concert halls and opera houses, his bulky figure, snowy white hair and old-fashioned hearing aid doing nothing to detract from his role as the Grand Old Man of English music, the link between Elgar and Benjamin Britten.

FANTASIA ON A THEME OF THOMAS TALLIS (1910)

A work for strings that could be nothing but English

A quintessential piece of English music, the *Tallis* Fantasy was introduced at the Three Choirs Festival in Gloucester in 1910. The theme is the third of eight tunes that Tallis composed in 1567 for the Metrical Psalter of Matthew Parker, Archbishop of Canterbury. Vaughan Williams uses a string orchestra divided into two, and a string quartet (played by the leaders of each group) to achieve an antiphonal effect, a popular device in 16th-century music where two distinct groups played in response to each other, a kind of Tudor stereo set-up. This was the work that finally emancipated English music from Continental influence.

If you like this, try: Vaughan Williams's Serenade to Music • Elgar's Serenade for strings • Tippett's Concerto for double string orchestra

The recording

ALLEGRI QUARTET
SINFONIA OF LONDON /
SIR JOHN BARBIROLLI
⊙ EMI 567240-2 + ▷

A classic recording that has been a top recommendation for years. Barbirolli's humane and wonderfully warm account of the *Tallis* Fantasia has a passion and intensity that is quite irresistible. The spatial division between solo quartet and full string orchestra is beautifully handled by the EMI engineers. The couplings, of music by Elgar and more Vaughan Williams, are equally superb.

THE LARK ASCENDING
(1914, rev 1920)

Music that evokes the wide open spaces of an empty sky

There are few who have not fallen under the spell of this ethereal fantasy for solo violin and orchestra. It is a musical translation of the poem of the same name by George Meredith (1828-1909) which begins: "He rises and begins to round, He drops the silver chain of sound, Of many links without a break, In chirrup, whistle, slur and shake…" The violin soars above the discreet orchestral accompaniment. There is a folk-like central section after which the violin/lark again takes flight. Vaughan Williams wrote the work for the English violinist Marie Hall and she played the first performance in London in 1921, with the British Symphony Orchestra under Adrian Boult.

If you like this, try: Sibelius's Serenades • Chausson's Meditation from Thaïs • Svendsen's Romance • Tavener's The Protecting Veil • Saint-Saëns's The Swan

The recording

TASMIN LITTLE
BBC SYMPHONY ORCHESTRA /
SIR ANDREW DAVIS
⊙ Apex 0927-49584-2 + ▷

Coupled with an alternative performance of the *Tallis* Fantasia and the Sixth Symphony, Tasmin Little turns in a ravishing account of *The Lark Ascending*, rhapsodic and sounding almost improvised. Sir Andrew Davis is an inspired Vaughan Williams conductor, and he draws some quite splendid playing from the BBC Symphony Orchestra.

VW ESSENTIALS

Fantasia on Greensleeves (1934)

This short instrumental piece, scored for harp, flute and strings, is made up of two folk songs: *Greensleeves* (an Elizabethan melody of unknown authorship) and *Lovely Joan*, a tune which VW himself came across in Norfolk in 1908. VW also used *Greensleeves* in his 1929 opera *Sir John in Love* (sung by Mistress Ford when she visits Sir John Falstaff).

Serenade to Music (1938)

Among the earliest champions of VW's music was the redoubtable Sir Henry Wood, co-founder of the Promenade Concerts and one of the leading figures in British musical life for more than half a century. For Sir Henry's Golden Jubilee Concert at the Royal Albert Hall in October 1938, VW composed this setting of Lorenzo's speech from Shakespeare's *The Merchant of Venice*. The Serenade is dedicated to Wood "in grateful memory of his services to music" and is surely one of the finest of any Shakespeare settings, the magical orchestral introduction setting the nocturnal mood, followed by the solo voices of 16 British singers with whom Sir Henry had been associated.

Symphony No 6 in E minor (1947, rev 1950)

One of the finest symphonies of the 20th century and among his greatest works, Vaughan Williams's Sixth was composed when he was 75 years old. The war and post-war period reverberate throughout the symphony, its four movements played without a break, reflecting the anguish and tragedy, turmoil and terror of the previous years. The symphony ends with some of the most serene music you'll ever hear (the longest section), "a whisper from beginning to end", ebbing away into uncertain optimism and "a stillness made audible".

SYMPHONY NO 5
(1938-43 rev. 1951)

Perhaps the greatest of Vaughan Williams's nine symphonies

Generally held to be the finest of Vaughan Williams's nine symphonies, the Fifth is dedicated to Sibelius and draws on ideas from the music VW had been working on for many years for his opera (or "morality" as he preferred to call it) *The Pilgrim's Progress*, eventually completed in 1951. Only the ghostly second movement (*Scherzo*) has no connection with the opera. All four movements of this tranquil, introspective masterpiece have a unanimity of mood: "it seems to fill the whole world with its song of good will," wrote one reviewer after Vaughan Williams himself conducted its first performance at a Promenade concert in June 1943.

137

The recording

LONDON SYMPHONY ORCHESTRA / RICHARD HICKOX

⊙ Chandos CHAN9666 + ➵

The LSO's VW symphony cycle that was sadly curtailed by Richard Hickox's tragically early death was shaping up into a thing of wonder. Together these superb British musicians tapped into a vein of poetry that created performances of an amazing radiance. The LSO's playing is outstanding and Chandos's engineering made the most of the huge dynamic range of the orchestra. A glorious disc.

If you like this, try: Vaughan Williams's A London Symphony • Vaughan Williams's Second String Quartet • Elgar's Symphony No 2 • Moeran's Symphony

Plácido Domingo
Tenor and conductor
A musical all-rounder,
superb as Verdi's Otello
(page 141) and very fine
in the German repertoire as
Wagner's Tristan (page 144)

ILLUSTRATION • BRUCE EMMETT

GIUSEPPE VERDI

Born Le Roncole 1813 **Died** Milan 1901

Verdi was never a theoretician or academic, though he was quite able to write a perfectly poised fugue if he felt inclined. What makes him, with Puccini, the most popular of all opera composers is the ability to dream up glorious melodies with an innate understanding of the human voice, to express himself directly, to understand how the theatre works, and to score with technical brilliance, colour and originality.

Unassailably one of the two or three greatest of all opera composers, Verdi was the son of a village inn-keeper and began his long musical career as an organist. It was not until 1839 that he had his first taste of success with his second opera *Oberto*, but between 1838 and 1840 he was faced with the awful tragedy of losing his two young children and his beloved young wife Margherita, the daughter of his early benefactor Antonio Barezzi.

Un giorno di regno (1840), a comic opera, was a failure and convinced Verdi he should abandon his operatic ambitions but the impresario Merelli persuaded him to undertake a fourth work, this time using the biblical subject of Nabucodonosor – or Nebuchadnezzar – (later shortened to *Nabucco*) (1841). It was a turning point in Verdi's career and also for Italian opera. Though still much influenced by Rossini and Donizetti, Verdi was hailed as the successor to Bellini and Donizetti, and his fame spread throughout Italy.

Between 1842 and 1850 he produced a further 12 operas with varying degrees of success but between 1851 and 1853 came three which would make his name immortal: *Rigoletto*, *Il Trovatore* and *La Traviata*. By the age of 40 he had eclipsed Meyerbeer as the most acclaimed living composer of opera. After these, triumph followed triumph with *Les Vêpres siciliennes* (1854), *Simon Boccanegra* (1857) and *Un ballo in maschera* in 1859, the year in which he married his long-time love, the soprano Giuseppina Strepponi.

Verdi was a fervent supporter of the Risorgimento and in the 1860s sat for five years as a deputy in that part of Italy already unified. Verdi, however, disliked direct involvement with politics and withdrew from the first Italian parliament (he was made a Senator in 1874, an honorary office which made no demands on him). During the summers, he and Giuseppina lived on a huge farm in Sant'Agata, enjoying a simple peasant existence. The winters were spent in their palatial home in Genoa. After *La forza del destino* (1862) came his flawed masterpiece *Don Carlos* (1867) and in 1870 *Aida*. The death in 1873 of the Italian poet and patriot Manzoni prompted Verdi to write his *Messa da Requiem*. Then, for the next 13 years, he retired to the country and wrote nothing.

It would have been reasonable to expect no more but in 1887 he entered a notable Indian summer with *Otello* and *Falstaff*, completed at the age of 79. After Giuseppini died in 1897, Verdi gradually lost the will to live. His sight and hearing deteriorated and after that suffered paralysis, but, setting aside 2,500,000 lire, he founded the Casa di Riposo per Musicisti in Milan, a home for aged musicians. It is still in operation. In 1898 he composed his last work, the *Four Sacred Songs*. In the Grand Hotel, Milan, he died from a sudden stroke at the age of 87. A quarter of a million people followed his funeral cortège on the way to his final resting place in the grounds of the Casa di Riposa.

LA TRAVIATA
(1853)
The fallen woman who sacrifices everything for love and is redeemed

The literal translation of the title, "The Fallen Woman" or "The Wayward Woman", is never used. The opera is based on the play (derived from the novel) *La Dame aux Camélias* by Alexandre Dumas fils about the legendary Parisian courtesan Marie Duplessis who died from tuberculosis in 1847 aged 23. In the opera she is called Violetta Valéry, the fallen woman who sacrifices everything for love and is thereby redeemed. Today, the opera is so much a part of the international repertoire that it's easy to forget what a revolutionary piece it was when it first appeared.

If you like this, try: Verdi's Il trovatore • Verdi's Un ballo in maschera • Puccini's Tosca • Puccini's La bohème • Bizet's Carmen • Massenet's Manon • Catalani's La Wally

140

MESSA DA REQUIEM
(1874)
'Verdi's best opera' – 'in church vestments'

Verdi's only masterpiece not intended for the stage has nevertheless been described as "Verdi's best opera" and "Verdi's latest opera, in church vestments". There is more than grain of truth in these verdicts. The death of his friend the poet and novelist Alessandro Manzoni in 1873 inspired Verdi to write this heartfelt and stirring setting of the Requiem Mass (sometimes called the Manzoni Requiem). Its success all over Europe was instant (Verdi took it on tour and played to full houses), combining the elegiac and spiritual (the tenor soloist's "Ingemisco", for instance) with the powerful and dramatic (try the "Dies irae" and "Tuba mirum" sections).

If you like this, try: Puccini's Messa di Gloria • Mozart's Requiem • Berlioz's Requiem • Elgar's Dream of Gerontius

VERDI ESSENTIALS

Rigoletto (1851)

The story of the hunchback jester Rigoletto, whose daughter Gilda is seduced by the libidinous Duke of Mantua. Its five best known numbers are often performed separately enforcing the mistaken view that they are "set pieces" and not integrated into the drama but "La donna è mobile", "Quest' o quella", "Caro nome", "Pari siamo" and the great Quartet (the finest in all opera) are all germane to the action and characterisation, incomparable examples of musical and dramatic veracity.

Il trovatore (1853)

"The Troubadours" was the most popular opera of the 19th century but, ironically, has one of the most implausible and imponderable plots of any opera. It says something for Verdi's skill that its narrative has never affected its hold on audiences for he provides a wonderfully varied musical feast, the roles of the four principal characters providing a veritable encyclopaedia of the vocal arts.

Aida (1871)

The final magnificent work of Verdi's second period in which every element of his art is incorporated: sublime large-scale choruses and poignant arias, pageantry, dance, spectacle, exoticism, it's all here, confirming Verdi (if confirmation were needed) as one of the great musical dramatists of history. The theme, once more, is doomed love – Radames, a Captain of the Egyptian guard falls for Aida, an Ethiopian slave. To her, Radames sings one of the great tenor arias "Celeste Aida" ("Heavenly Aida"); the other memorable moments are Aida's "Ritorna vincitor" ("Return victorious") and "O patria mia" ("O my native land") and their final duet before being entombed alive "O terra, addio" ("O Earth, farewell"). And who can resist the Grand March (Act 2) – with or without elephants?

OTELLO (1887)

Arguably Verdi's finest opera and his greatest achievement

Arguably Verdi's finest opera and his greatest achievement. Nearly 15 years separate *Aida* from *Otello* and Verdi felt increasingly as he grew older that he could not surpass the achievement of *Aida*. "Let's quit while I'm ahead" seems to have been his thinking, for Wagner's operas were now dominating the opera world and, though he admired Wagner, Verdi knew that such methods were not for him. Having been seduced by Boito's treatment of Shakespeare's *Othello*, however, the old man set to work. Even more than *Aida*, the musical and dramatic elements were welded indivisibly together. Passages to look out for are "Credo in un Dio crudel" ("I believe in a cruel God") in Act 2, Desdemona's moving "Salce, salce, salce" ("Oh Willow, willow, willow") and "Ave Maria" in Act 4.

141

The recording

PLÁCIDO DOMINGO; CHERYL STUDER; OPÉRA-BASTILLE, PARIS / MYUNG-WHUN CHUNG

⊙ DG 439 805-2GH2 + ▣→

Domingo is in superb voice – a great Otello caught at the height of his powers; the sound seems golden as never before. Yet at the same time, it's a voice that's being more astutely deployed. Chung's conducting is almost disarmingly vital – the score sounds very brilliant. Studer's is a carefully drawn portrait of a chaste and sober-suited lady.

If you like this, try: Verdi's Falstaff • Puccini's Turandot • Leoncavallo's Pagliacci • Mascagni's Cavalleria rusticana

THE FOUR SEASONS
(1725)

He created some of the most innovative music of the age

Vivaldi was the prototype of the modern virtuoso, bewitching his audiences with his technical prowess and, as a composer, creating some of the most original and innovative music of the age. The four concertos that make up *The Four Seasons* are just part of a collection of 12 published in 1725 under the collective title of *Il cimento dell'armonia e dell'inventione* ("The Contest between Harmony and Invention"). Each of *The Seasons* has three movements (fast-slow-fast) and are rich in musical characterisations: No 1 "Spring" has the goatherd's trusty dog barking (the viola); No 2 "Summer" has bird-song and a frightening summer storm; No 3 "Autumn" has a drunken harvest celebration and a stag hunt; No 4 "Winter" presents the chattering cold and, in the lovely slow movement, rain dripping on the trees while the fortunate ones are sat next to a warm fire.

With Antonio Vivaldi, Italian Baroque music reached its zenith. The prosperous, cultivated world of contemporary Venice shines through all his works, composed with innate craftsmanship.

Vivaldi (1678-1741) was born in Venice at a time when the city was the musical capital of Europe. His father was a violinist at San Marco and his son inherited his gift for the instrument as well as his red hair. When he was 15 he began training for the priesthood and was ordained in 1703, hence his nickname "The Red Priest". The Church remained a useful backcloth, but it seems that his priestly duties were never taken terribly seriously.

What he took only slightly more seriously was his position as *maestro di violino* (and later superintendent) of the Conservatorio dell'Ospedale della Pietá, one of the most famous musical centres in Venice, founded for the care and education of orphan girls. Vivaldi took up the post in 1704. The following year saw the first publication of his music. The next two decades were incredibly productive and he established himself as one of the foremost violinists and composers in Europe: operas (at least one a year between 1713 and 1738, sometimes three or four) and instrumental works, including his two most famous sets of concerti (*L'Estro Armonico*, Op 3 and *The Four Seasons*, Op 8).

The 1730s saw his powers wane. The Church authorities took action against Vivaldi because of his lapsed priesthood and his contract with La Pietá was not renewed. His music began to fall out of favour and he left for Vienna in 1740, possibly with the intention of seeking a post with the Imperial Court of Vienna. It was not to be. The illustrious Vivaldi, now ill and poverty-stricken, died some months later and was buried in a pauper's grave.

142

The recording

GIULIANO CARMIGNOLA; VENICE BAROQUE ORCHESTRA / ANDREA MARCON

⊙ Sony Classical SK51352 + ⮫

Giuliano Carmignola has a keen narrative flair. He knows the musical period, understands principles of embellishment and doesn't hesitate to enrich his performances with added colour and with rhythmic thrust. He's aided by the equally inventive playing of the orchestra, and the result is one of the most highly charged performances of this ever-popular work.

If you like this, try: Vivaldi's La Stravaganza • Vivaldi's Gloria • Bach's Brandenburg Concertos • Haydn's The Seasons

RICHARD WAGNER

Born Leipzig 1813 **Died** Venice 1883

No composer has had so deep an influence on the course of his art, before or since. Entrepreneur, philosopher, poet, conductor, one of the key composers in history and most remarkable men of the 19th century, Wagner knew he was a genius. He was also an unpleasant, egocentric and unscrupulous human being.

The salient factors of his early career are that, save for six months of counterpoint lesson, he was virtually self-taught; his first works, two orchestral overtures, were premiered in Leipzig in 1829 before he had had any formal training; he married a pretty young actress named Minna Planer in 1836 and the two of them spent much of the next decade fleeing their debtors while Wagner held various minor conducting posts and composed. By the time he had written *Rienzi* (1840) and *The Flying Dutchman* (1841) he was director of the Dresden Opera, raising performance standards to unprecedented heights. 1845 saw the premiere of *Tannhäuser*. By 1848 he had almost completed a third operatic masterpiece, *Lohengrin*.

Wagner was forced to flee Germany in 1849 after siding with revolutionaries during an uprising in Saxony and lived in exile in Zurich for the next 13 years. Here he formulated his radical ideas about opera and the "music of the future": the concept of "music drama" involving a synthesis of all the arts. The plan that began to occupy his mind was a giant project of four dramas in which all his theories would be realised, an opera cycle called *The Ring of the Nibelungs*. It took him a quarter of a century to complete it. While working on *The Ring*, Wagner interrupted his labours with two other music dramas, *Tristan and Isolde* (1859) and *Die Meistersinger* (1867).

After a string of affairs, in 1862 Wagner fell in love with Cosima, the daughter of Franz Liszt and the wife of his friend and champion, the pianist and conductor Hans von Bülow. Four years later, Cosima deserted Bülow and set up house with Wagner. Throughout, Bülow remained devoted to Wagner and wrote approvingly to Cosima: "You have preferred to devote your life and the treasures of your mind to one who is my superior."

In the meantime, a political amnesty allowed Wagner to return to Germany in 1860 (Saxony in 1862). Four years later, King Ludwig II of Bavaria ascended the throne and invited Wagner to Munich, promising him unlimited support for all his projects. Between 1865 and 1870 Munich was host to the world premieres of *Tristan and Isolde*, *Die Meistersinger*, *Das Rheingold* and *Die Walkürie* (the last two being the first completed sections of *The Ring*). In 1871, Wagner announced plans for a purpose-built theatre where his works could be mounted under ideal conditions, produced to his own specifications. The council of the little Bavarian town of Bayreuth offered him a site. The Bayreuth Festival Theatre was unveiled on August 13, 1876. The opening performance was the first complete presentation of *The Ring* cycle. In 1878 Wagner finished his last opera or "consecrational play" *Parsifal*. The same year he suffered the first of a series of heart attacks, a fatal one in Venice. His body was brought back to Bayreuth where it was buried in a vault in the garden of his villa to the strains of the funeral march from *Götterdämmerung*.

143

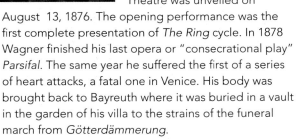

TRISTAN UND ISOLDE
(1856-59)

A turning point in music as well as in the history of opera

The opera, a psychological music-drama, is of great importance in the history of music and its evolution. To musicologists, Wagner's use of chromaticism to express the themes of love and death heralded the break-up of tonality and pointed the way forward to composers like Schoenberg. It is the starting point of modern music and its very opening, the famous Prelude, breaks with tradition by being not written in any definable key. There isn't much in the way of dramatic action, but if it is not approached casually and you have a chance to study some of the background to it, *Tristan* becomes a remarkable, even overwhelming experience. Based on Arthurian legend, the opera tells the story of the doomed lovers Tristan and Isolde and inspires Wagner's most sensual and passionate love music: the Liebestod, Isolde's final and ecstatic declaration of love, is the opera's crowning glory.

144

The recording

PLÁCIDO DOMINGO; NINA STEMME; ROYAL OPERA HOUSE ORCHESTRA / ANTONIO PAPPANO

⊙ EMI 558006-2 + ↦

You might be forgiven for assuming that the star of this recording is Plácido Domingo – and he gives an ardent, and tireless performance (aided by the studio conditions). But the true stars are the Isolde of Nina Stemme, who sings with radiant tone and a

total sympathy for the role, and Antonio Pappano, who conducts with a truly grand sweep and draws some staggering playing from his Covent Garden orchestra. The remainder of the cast is excellent, making this a fine modern version.

HELEN LYON/EMI CLASSICS

If you like this, try: Wagner's Wesendonk-Lieder • Wagner's Parsifal • Debussy's Pelléas et Mélisande • Schoenberg's Gurrelieder • Mahler's Symphony No 10 • Martin's Le vin herbé

WAGNER ESSENTIALS

Lohengrin (1845-48)

Opera connoisseurs rate this as Wagner's first true masterpiece. The story revolves round Elsa of Brabant accused of murdering her brother and who dreams of a knight defending her from the charge. A mysterious knight does appear and will stay as long as she never asks his name or whence he came. It emerges that he is Lohengrin, son of Parsifal, keeper of the Holy Grail. Wagner makes some bold developments, including associating different musical themes with certain characters.

Die Meistersinger von Nürnberg (1845 and 1861-67)

The Mastersingers of Nuremberg's allegorical story is based on fact. Wagner took the subject of the medieval literary and musical movement cultivated by middle-class trade guilds whose members were called Mastersingers. The most famous of these was Hans Sachs who lived in Nuremberg from 1494 to 1576. The magnificent Overture, often heard independently, is a masterly piece of writing using many of the themes from the opera.

Der Ring des Nibelungen (1848-74)

One of man's greatest creative achievements. Its length alone, never mind its dramatic and musical content, makes it unique. The libretti of the four operas were written in reverse order. Having become interested in the North European sagas, Wagner's first literary text, written in 1848, was Götterdammerung. Realising that the story needed an introduction, he then wrote Siegfried (1851). This in turn was prefaced by Die Walküre explaining Siegfried's parentage. Finally, as a prologue, he wrote Das Rheingold. The whole cycle lasts 15 hours and is played over four evenings.

DECCA

SIEGFRIED IDYLL
(1870)
A lullaby that was Wagner's gift to his bride...and the world

Cosima Wagner was born on Christmas Day 1837, the daughter of Franz Liszt and the Countess d'Agoult. For her 33rd birthday she received a birthday present which the whole world has been able to share with gratitude, the *Siegfried Idyll*. This eloquent lullaby for chamber orchestra was conceived in secrecy by Wagner for his new bride and young son Siegfried. On Christmas morning 1870, at half past seven, 15 musicians assembled quietly on the stairs leading to Cosima's bedroom and played this "beautiful and intolerably poignant serenade". The themes are drawn from *Siegfried*, the third opera in *The Ring* cycle (particularly the love music from Act 3), but also quotes the old German cradle song "Schlaf, mein Kind". It's Wagner at his most intimate and charming.

145

The recording

VIENNA PHILHARMONIC ORCHESTRA / SIR GEORG SOLTI

⊙ Decca 475 850-2 + ▷➔

This performance of Wagner's delightful *Siegfried Idyll* is one of the loveliest recordings Solti ever made. Putting his sometimes hard-driven style to one side, he allows this exquisite birthday present to unfurl with an elegance and poetry that is simply entrancing.

Had Cosima heard a performance

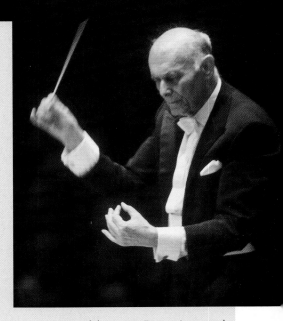

as unforced and natural as this, then her birthday would surely have started on an unrepeatable note. Decca's sound brings out the sweetness and charm of the Viennese strings to perfection.

If you like this, try: Mahler's Adagietto (Symphony No 5) • Dvořák's Serenade for strings • Elgar's Serenade for Strings • Schoenberg's Verklärte Nacht • R Strauss's Metamophosen

BELSHAZZAR'S FEAST

(1931)

Real painting in music

Although officially labelled "cantata", this was the most significant English oratorio since Elgar's *The Dream of Gerontius*. Originally commissioned in 1929 by the BBC who asked for a small-scale choral work, by 1930 the work had grown so large that the BBC released Walton from his contract. It requires a solo baritone, chorus and orchestra plus an expanded brass section, the latter supposedly in response to Sir Thomas Beecham's remark before the first performance in Leeds: "As you'll never hear the thing again, why not throw in a couple of brass bands?" *Belshazzar's Feast* is a thrilling and powerful experience, "a paean of praise for the god of gold", and Walton's choral writing, in the best Anglican tradition, is masterly.

146

The recording

BRYN TERFEL
BBC SINGERS; BBC SYMPHONY CHORUS AND ORCHESTRA / SIR ANDREW DAVIS

⊙ Apex 0927 44394-2 + ⯈

Recorded live at the 1994 Last Night of the Proms, this is a performance that has a very special atmosphere. Bryn Terfel is a real stage animal and you can sense that the occasion drew a very special drama from him: his delivery is terrific, his diction characteristically crystal-clear. Add to that orchestral playing of the first order, a conductor who loves this music and you have a superb CD at budget price.

If you like this, try: Walton's Symphony No 1 • Elgar's The Dream of Gerontius • Elgar's Sea Pictures • Britten's War Requiem • Bernstein's Chichester Psalms

Walton's language, characterised by pungent orchestration, driving energy and virile rhythms, yet with an unmistakable Elgarian Englishness, makes his music easily accessible.

At the age of 10, Walton (1902-83) won a place as a chorister at Christ Church Cathedral School, Oxford, and matriculated from Christ College at the amazingly early age of 16. While at Oxford he met the Sitwell family who took him under their wing. For the next decade and more, Walton lived with them in their houses in Chelsea and Italy as a sort of adopted brother.

He was only 19 when he composed the work that first brought his name to public attention, *Façade*. It consisted of a series of abstract poems by Edith Sitwell declaimed through a megaphone behind a curtain to the accompaniment of Walton's irreverent, brilliantly-scored music. After such hedonistic high-spirits, Walton soon proved that he was capable of great things with his Viola Concerto, the dramatic cantata *Belshazzar's Feast* and his fizzing Symphony No1.

Walton composed his first film score in 1934 (*Escape Me Never*) and discovered a medium to which his lyrico-dramatic gifts were ideally suited. It was while working on the film of *As You Like It* (1936) that he first met Laurence Olivier and the three Shakespeare films in which he subsequently collaborated with Olivier, *Henry V*, *Hamlet* and *Richard III*, put Walton in a class of his own as a film composer.

He wrote little during the decade after the Second World War, married the Argentine Susana Gil in 1948 in Buenos Aires and shortly after settled on the island of Ischia off the coast of Naples. His opera *Troilus and Cressida* (1954), Cello Concerto (1956) and Second Symphony (1960) were all coolly received by the critics. By the time he died, his music was once again coming back into fashion.